100 Ideas for Secondary Teachers:

Tutor Time

Other titles in the 100 Ideas for Secondary Teachers series:

100 Ideas for Secondary Teachers:

Tutor Time

Molly Potter

B L O O M S B U R Y
LONDON · OXFORD · NEW YORK · NEW DELHI · SYDNEY

Bloomsbury Education
An imprint of Bloomsbury Publishing Plc

50 Bedford Square
London
WC1B 3DP
UK

1385 Broadway
New York
NY 10018
USA

www.bloomsbury.com

Bloomsbury is a registered trade mark of Bloomsbury Publishing Plc

First published 2016

British Library Cataloguing-in-Publication Data
A catalogue record for this book is available from the British Library.

ISBN:
PB 9781472925022
ePub 9781472925046
ePDF 9781472925039

Library of Congress Cataloging-in-Publication Data
A catalog record for this book is available from the Library of Congress.

10 9 8 7 6 5 4 3 2 1

Typeset by Newgen Knowledge Works (P) Ltd., Chennai, India
Printed and bound
by CPI Group (UK) Ltd, Croydon, CRO 4YY

This book is produced using paper that is made from wood grown in
managed, sustainable forests. It is natural, renewable and recyclable.
The logging and manufacturing processes conform to the
environmental regulations of the country of origin.

To view more of our titles please visit www.bloomsbury.com

Contents

Acknowledgements   ix
Introduction   xi
How to use this book   xii

**Routines and procedures – setting up
what's needed for things to run smoothly**   **1**
1 What do I do in tutor time?   2
2 Scool rools   3
3 Get ground rules   4
4 What shall we do?   6
5 Uniform   7
6 Any announcements?   8
7 Taking in notes   9
8 One to one   10
9 Late again   11
10 Just for you!   12

**Pastoral care – ideas to help support a
registration tutor in their pastoral care role** **13**
11 Self-esteem   14
12 Communicate   15
13 Help!   16
14 Safeguarding   17
15 Study difficulties   18
16 Mediate!   19
17 Beat bad behaviour   20
18 Anti-bullying   21
19 Homework support   22
20 Friendship difficulties   24
21 Target setting   25
22 E safety   26

**Community building – activities to help
your tutor group bond**   **27**
23 How well do we know you?   28
24 Negotiate   29
25 Two truths and a lie   30
26 Connect with Venn   31
27 No giggling!   32
28 What's the question?   33

29	Secret best friend	34
30	Charity work	35
31	Down it goes!	36
32	Group gazette	37
33	A, B, or C?	38

Active learning techniques – tools for exploring different issues   **39**

34	Four words	40
35	Graffiti wall	41
36	Quick to draw	42
37	I agree... or not	43
38	Top ten tips	44
39	Under the hammer	45
40	World's worst, world's best	46
41	Hot seat	47
42	Recipe writing	48
43	Order! Order!	49
44	Step forward	50

Teen issues – PSHE style activities covering issues relevant to teenagers   **53**

45	Who am I?	54
46	Advice, please!	56
47	Dilemmas	57
48	Peer influence	58
49	A culture of compliments	60
50	Whatever!	61
51	Puberty	62
52	It's a risk	63
53	I'm hideous	64
54	Hard health choices	65
55	Street safety	66
56	Motiv8	67
57	Stress and strain	68
58	When I grow up...	69
59	Changing for the better	70
60	Assert!	71
61	Dealing with insults	72
62	It's how I feel	73
63	Loads-a-friends	74

I think... – exploring and developing attitudes, values and opinions   **75**

| 64 | I've changed my mind | 76 |
| 65 | I like that; I don't like that | 78 |

66 What's important to you? — 79
67 A walk around town — 80
68 Effective discussion and debate — 82
69 Happy, happy? — 83
70 We're not equal — 84
71 Values or opinions — 85
72 What do we need? — 86
73 Is it wrong? — 88

Thinking and creative fun – activities to engage students in creative thinking and pondering! — **89**
74 That's unusual! — 90
75 The longest list — 91
76 Memorise it! — 92
77 Proverbs — 93
78 Pass it on! — 94
79 Observation — 95
80 I have control — 96
81 Ordinary, extraordinary and extra-extraordinary — 97
82 Excuses, excuses! — 98
83 Hands — 99
84 Anagram hunt — 100
85 Wordplay — 101

Media – developing a discerning eye for the media — **103**
86 What messages! — 104
87 Newsworthy? — 105
88 Headlines — 106
89 Different points of view — 107
90 Fame and fortune — 108
91 Adverts — 109
92 Topical — 110

General knowledge – activities with factual information to improve general knowledge — **113**
93 Which language — 114
94 When was that invented? — 115
95 Left or right? — 116
96 When was that then? — 117
97 Animal trivia — 118
98 It's legal — 119
99 Place name detective — 120
100 Historical fame — 121

Acknowledgements

Firstly, I would like to thank my many colleagues from the various educational environments I have worked at over the years. While I am an 'ideas' person, I have no doubt that some of the activities in this book have been influenced by people I have worked with. In this respect I would particularly like to thank Anna Sims, Sue Astbury, Marian Fox, and Rosemary Games.

I would also like to thank Suki Dell and Andrei Mazzei for scrutinising any active learning techniques I used in training sessions and giving me valuable feedback. They both helped me develop some of the ideas in this book.

Last, but certainly not least, I need to thank my adorable family (Andy, Maddy and Jed) for their patience when dealing with an oddball mother who regularly disappears for sustained periods of time to tap away at the keyboard and then shouts out random comments like, 'Just 96 more ideas to go!'

Introduction

The role of form tutor varies from school to school, but responsibilities that often fall to tutors can include:

- The registration of your form
- Dissemination of information
- Instilling good habits and routines
- Monitoring students' progress and supporting those who struggle
- Providing support for students who have behavioural difficulties and for the colleagues who work with them
- Ensuring the general wellbeing of your tutees
- Being the key adult for each member of your form and a point of contact for parents/carers when issues arise
- Initiating activities that will broaden the curriculum of your tutees
- Delivering non-statutory PSHE lessons.

In short, your responsibilities to these students are far more holistic than your responsibilities to the students to whom you deliver your curriculum subject. This book aims to help you fulfil this role more successfully. Not only does it provide general tips to help you in a pastoral care role, it also provides many, engaging registration-time activities that usually require very little, or no, preparation.

Some of the ideas in this book are simple and straightforward, or are one-off pieces of advice. Others could be used repeatedly, or developed considerably further. It is hoped that these more complex ideas will provide inspiration when it comes to delivering a well-rounded 'extra' curriculum that will help students: develop values and opinions; engage in creative thinking; consider issues pertinent to teenagers; develop a discerning eye for messages given out by the media; develop general knowledge and an enjoyment of discussion.

This book is intended to be dipped in and out of. Some ideas might jump out at you; others you might leave alone but, given the number of ideas in this book, hopefully every tutor will find something meaningful, whatever their approach to teaching.

How to use this book

This book includes quick, easy, practical ideas and guidance for you to dip in and out of, to help you provide for secondary school students during tutor time sessions.

Each idea includes:

- A catchy title, easy to refer to and share with your colleagues
- An opening quote – either from a practitioner, parent or student describing their experience or something that has led to the idea
- A summary of the idea in bold, making it easy to flick through the book and identify an idea you want to use at a glance
- A step-by-step guide to implementing the idea.

Each idea also includes one or more of the following:

Teaching tip

Practical tips and advice on how best to run the activity or put the idea into practice, and what pit-falls to avoid.

Taking it further

Ideas and advice for how to extend the idea.

Bonus idea ★

There are 38 bonus ideas in this book that are extra-exciting, extra-original, and extra-interesting!

Involving parents

Tips on how to get parents involved in their children's learning.

Share how you use these ideas and find out what other practitioners have done using **#100ideas**.

Routines and procedures – setting up what's needed for things to run smoothly

Part 1

What do I do in tutor time?

"Get a routine in place as soon as possible. Be clear about that routine and it will help the sessions run smoothly."

It's important to set out clear routines and expectations during your first meeting with your tutor group. They will need to know what will happen in their time with you and what you will expect from them.

In the first few sessions with your tutor group:

- Explain how you will expect them to enter the room (quietly) and where you would like them to sit (you could allocate designated places or allow them to sit wherever they like).
- Explain your role. What will you be available for? What can you support pupils with? What will you need to do each morning? What other activities will happen in tutor time (e.g. PSHE sessions)? What information do you have about each student (e.g. behaviour and academic achievement)?
- Explain the school rules and the relevant parts of your school behaviour policy.
- Explain that it is important that the register is accurate as it is a legal document.
- Set up any systems or procedures that you will be using (e.g. information sharing, taking in notes, rewards and sanctions you might use, how you will follow up when a pupil is absent or late).
- Explain the use of wall displays designated for tutor group use and information.
- Explain how students can have one-to-one meetings with you if they feel they need it.

Scool Rools

"Rules exist for good reasons. A place like a school needs rules to help it run efficiently and safely."

As a form tutor, you will be responsible for helping your form group to acknowledge, understand and adhere to the school rules. It is a good idea to use form time to explore school rules and help students understand the need for each rule.

There are a number of ways to explore school rules:

- Ask students to turn each rule into a road sign using symbols to communicate the point.
- Ask students to deliver the rules without using words – other students have to guess the rule they are demonstrating.
- Ask students to sort the rules into categories based on why the rule is needed. The categories could include:

  o the need to keep everyone safe;
  o the need for everyone to feel respected;
  o the need to make sure learning happens as efficiently as possible;
  o the need to keep things fair.

- Take each rule in turn and ask students 'what difficulties and problems would arise if people did not follow this rule?'
- Ask pupils to order the rules starting with those they consider the most important to those they consider the least important. Ask them to explain their reasoning.
- Ask pupils to turn each of the school rules into a rhyming couplet. (e.g. You really don't want to be running in school, Or you could trip and look like a fool.)

Involving parents

Ask students to discuss the school rules with their parents/carers and collect a comment the parent/carer made about the rules to share in a later session.

3

Get ground rules

"School rules are one thing, but what about making your form group a safe and happy place to be?"

Every school has rules that focus on safety, respect for other people/property and optimising learning. Ground rules are about making a group a comfortable place to be and are best developed with input from the people in that group. Develop a set of ground rules with your form group when you first get together.

There are a lot of different ways to develop ground rules. The best methods allow everyone to contribute. You could use any of the following methods to create ground rules that aim to make your form group a welcoming and inclusive environment.

- Introduce a fictional person: 'Sam'. Explain that Sam is nervous about coming into the room. Ask students what they could do to make him/her feel less nervous. List their suggestions. These can form the basis of ground rules.
- Ask pupils to list a set of behaviours that they think are unattractive or make them feel uncomfortable or unwelcome. The opposites of this list can be a set of ground rules.
- Use the following question prompts:

  o When you are discussing an issue with someone, what could they do that might make you feel uncomfortable, and what helps to make you feel comfortable?
  o What is important when the class is discussing an issue as a whole class?
  o What can people do to show they are listening to you properly?
  o How can someone disagree with you without leaving you feeling deflated or angry?
  o What makes you feel respected?

- o How can we ensure everyone gets a chance to speak if they wish to?
- Give the following words to groups of three students:
  RESPECT   AFFIRMATION   EQUALITY CHALLENGE   SAFETY   FUN
- Check they know what all the words mean. Ask pupils to discuss ground rules that will help everyone feel comfortable in your form group and relate to the words they have been given. After ten minutes, ask them to share their ideas.
- Read the text, 'I did not enjoy my day', and ask students to highlight all the parts where Max was made to feel bad or uncomfortable. Ask pairs of students to write down some rules that would prevent Max from feeling the way he did (e.g. if someone asks for feedback – make it positive and constructive).

I did not enjoy my day

Max entered the classroom. Everyone stared at him. Poppy and Brian whispered to each other. Max sat down at his desk. Jane sat next to him, but she had her back turned. When Jane turned round, she made a joke about how messy his hair was. When Max said, 'That doesn't make me feel very good,' Jane just laughed at him.

During break-time, Max couldn't find anyone to talk to. Eventually Ben came talked to him about the football team, but Max felt he couldn't really get a word in. During maths, Max got stuck but the teacher appeared not to understand what it was Max was finding difficult and dismissed him. Things looked like they were going to get better in history, as Max was drawing a storyboard of the Battle of Hastings; but then the teacher told him that he he needed to finish it more quickly so he could write a version of the story out. He asked the teacher if he liked his drawing, but he said he thought it was just messy.

What shall we do?

"Letting students give their view of what should happen during registration time is great practice."

Involve your tutor group in deciding what should happen during registration and tutor time to enhance their 'buy in' to the sessions. A questionnaire is the most efficient way of doing this.

Early on in your time with the students in your tutor group, you could consult them about what they would like to see happen in their time with you. Create a questionnaire with the following questions for students to respond to:

- What rules specific to tutor time do you think would be a good idea?
- What do you think will happen in tutor group time?
- What support do you think a form tutor should give you?
- For what reasons do you think your form tutor should contact your parents/carers?
- What do you think should happen if your form tutor learns you are struggling with your school work?
- Would you like any of the following to happen in tutor time: e.g.:

  o the opportunity for students to deliver presentations on things that interest them;
  o PSHE lessons;
  o problem-solving sessions – to help with difficulties that individuals bring to the group;
  o literacy support;
  o session lead by students – where they set the group a task or puzzle;
  o sharing information about holidays;
  o team-building activities;
  o opportunities to speak with your form tutor individually;
  o opportunities to discuss current affairs topics;
  o opportunities to discuss school issues;
  o reviews of how you are doing at school;
  o any other ideas of what you would like included?

Bonus idea ★

You could ask your students to simply write what they most hope will happen in tutor group sessions and take their answers in.

Uniform

"The topic of school uniform can create a lot of debate and a lot of battles."

As a form tutor you will need to make expectations about uniform clear and police adherence to these. If you make your expectations clear from the outset policing will hopefully be less necessary.

Chances are, nearly all of your new form will turn up on their first day wearing the correct school uniform. However, this is still a good time to clarify what the school uniform is and to state that you hope that there will be little need for you to check that all students are in uniform each day.

To consider the issue of uniform with your students you could:

- Ask students to complete illustrated lists of 'acceptable' and 'unacceptable' clothes to wear at school.
- Ask students to produce a comical TV advert or a sales channel 'selling' the benefits of your particular school uniform. Encourage exaggeration!
- Ask every student to write something they like about their school uniform. Ask willing students to share what they have written.
- Debate the pros and cons of school uniform.
- Discuss the reasons why students might try to 'bend the rules' when it comes to uniform.
- Disclose the school's reasons for deciding to have a school uniform.
- Stress how boring you find addressing a student who is not wearing correct uniform and make clear what will happen if this occurs.

Involving parents

Create a standard black and white, labelled picture of a school uniform with spaces to indicate where a student has failed to achieve the correct uniform. You can use this as a standard letter to send to parents/ carers to minimise the time and energy you give to this issue.

Any announcements?

"A never-ending responsibility of the form tutor is disseminating information."

At the beginning of the day there is often important information you need to give to your students. Try out some other,fun methods of delivering this information to students.

To 'spice up' your announcements each morning (e.g. about upcoming events, cancelled activities and/or opportunities to volunteer) you could:

- Have several information monitors who you brief and let deliver the information students need.
- Get different students to doodle a 'poster' on scrap paper with the key information that needs to be shared and let them share it at the end of the form group session.
- Categorise the information (e.g. academic, practical arrangements in the school day, something interesting going on, reminders, a decision that needs to be made) and have a visual display of these categories. Stand by the visual reminders to deliver information.
- You could occasionally allow a student to deliver the information using hand signals alone – other students have to guess what the message is.
- Give three words relating to the information and see if students can guess what it is.
- Deliver information and ask students to give it a catchy or headline title.
- To check for engagement, you can ask students to raise their arms if they think the information is relevant to them.

Taking in notes

"It can be extremely busy, with a flurry of activity first thing, when there are lots of letters to take in."

A system that you can put in place that will reduce chaos in your registration sessions is to ask monitors to collect notes from other students.

Set up a system for notes being taken in by:

- Appointing responsible monitors to collect all notes and monies;
- Appointing at least four students for this role so that you are covered in the case of absence;
- Creating a book that includes all the names of the students in your tutor group. Each time a letter that requires a response is sent out, note it down so that the replies can be ticked off as they are returned.
- Providing a tray for pupils to place monies and notes in. Include paperclips so that reply slips can be grouped together when there are replies to different letters coming in.
- Giving monitors the responsibility of issuing reminders to students who have forgotten to bring forms in. These reminders can be a standard slip with a space to write the student's name, what they need to remember and the date/deadline for returning it.
- Asking your monitors to check that names are written on each reply. You could also ask your monitors to note the date the replies were received.

Bonus idea ★

You could provide an incentive to return letters and monies the following day by offering a reward or privilege for those who manage it five times in a row.

One to one

"Some students will have little to do with you, whereas others might need your support and guidance quite regularly."

It is important that you are available to your students, should they need you. You might have to initiate one-to-one sessions with students who are struggling academically or who have poor attendance; but it is also good practice to let your students know when and where they could reach you if problems arise.

Teaching tip

It is a good idea to give students some examples of the kind of issues they might need support with, so that they do not feel foolish about approaching you (e.g. bullying, school work difficulties, friendship difficulties, any difficulties at home affecting their ability to focus on school work, etc.)

Bonus idea ★

Childline offers free posters that advertise their confidential service. It is a good idea to have at least one of these on display in your classroom and to make reference to the organisation every now and then.

As a teacher, your day is always busy but making time for individual students in your tutor group can be achieved by:

- Holding 'drop-in' sessions at break times on one or two days a week – tell your students that you will always be in your class room during these times if they want to talk or ask for help with anything. Often students will not use this time and you will be able to get on with something else.
- Explaining that if a student needs you urgently, you can usually be found in your classroom for the first ten minutes at the end of every day.
- Providing a 'support box' where students can post written notes to you with any queries, difficulties or problems they are having. You could initially respond with a written reply, but also offer an appointment when the student could visit you and talk things through.
- Making sure your students know about the other pastoral support that is available to them from other individual members of staff in your school.

Late again

"Some students will struggle with punctuality more than others."

Make it clear to students from the outset that you expect them to arrive on time. Reflecting upon the issue of punctuality will reduce the likeliness of lateness.

Firstly, ask students to consider their ability to be punctual. Ask students if they are:

- Someone who always struggles to be on time;
- Always on time;
- If their punctuality depends upon where they have to be.

Next discuss the problems with lateness.

- In the register lateness is classified as an unauthorised absence;
- Missing important notices;
- Punctuality is a life skill – if you were late for work frequently you could possibly lose your job.

Explain the procedures that the school undertakes when a student is repeatedly late.

- How many times does a student need to be late for procedures to start?
- What happens?
- Are parents/carers involved?

Discuss reasons students give for being late, e.g.

- I was waiting for a friend.
- My alarm clock did not go off.
- I lost track of time.

Discuss tips for making lateness less likely.

- Set your alarm clock for an earlier time.
- Check that you have all you need for the morning and the school day the night before.
- Arrange a time by which you will leave without a friend if they have not turned up.
- Wear a watch!

Teaching tip

Always role model punctuality yourself!

Bonus idea ★

Get pupils to create lateness prevention posters with tips for punctuality!

Just for you!

"I like my role as a form tutor and I like to make my form feel welcome and looked after in my classroom."

Although you will mostly be teaching your subject in your classroom, it is a good to let your tutor group have some ownership of the room. Here are some suggestions for how you could achieve this.

Help your tutor group 'own' your classroom by:

- Dedicating a display board to your tutor group (to include notices, photos, anything impressive that has been produced by students in tutor time, etc.);
- Providing a box of useful things that students might have forgotten (like pencils, pens, etc.) for students to borrow;
- Asking students from your registration group to create an entertaining door sign for your classroom (e.g. including a picture of you, a catchphrase you use, pictures of things relating to your subject area etc.);
- Allowing your tutor group to help you with displays, handing out books, labeling cupboards, tidying, and sorting in your classroom. You can allocate monitors to complete different jobs each morning.
- Letting your tutor group make decisions about how the tables and seats are arranged;
- Creating a patchwork strip – students from your tutor group can decorate a 10 cm by 10 cm square of paper, this can then be added to a line of squares somewhere in the classroom. To make it visually interesting, insist that no white is left on the square. Over the year, they can choose to add to the strip or replace squares they completed previously.

> **Bonus idea** ★
>
> You could consult with your students about what they think of your room and take suggestions for how it could be improved.

Pastoral care
– ideas to
help support a
registration tutor
in their pastoral
care role

Part 2

Self-esteem

"Self-esteem makes us more resilient to the knocks we receive in life."

While the main influence on a young person's self-worth usually comes from their home life, school can have some impact. As a tutor you can boost your students' self-worth.

When possible, give positive phone-calls home – especially to the parents/carers of students who are not used to hearing positive things about their children.

You could boost your students' self-worth in the following ways:

- In a PSHE session, discuss self-esteem (or self-worth) with your students. How does a person with good self-worth approaches school (and life) differently to someone with low self-worth? How do people develop good self-esteem? Ask students to consider their own self-esteem.
- Discuss self-talk. Do your students put themselves down in their own heads? Explain that they can make this positive.
- Celebrate students' achievements and encourage them to state something that they are proud of. Some students will struggle with this so give them a list of things they might not have considered (e.g. maintained friendships, sporting achievements, punctuality)
- Give specific praise to individual students, e.g. 'I have noticed how helpful you are when your friends are upset.' This is more effective than vague praise as students will remember it for a long time.
- Ask students to choose three qualities that they possess from a set list. Qualities could include: supportive, hard working, responsible, organised, a good friend, determined, emotional, creative, sociable, a team-player, imaginative, articulate, optimistic, honest, calm, a good listener, enthusiastic, confident, independent, sense of humour, etc.

Communicate

"It's not easy to find time to communicate with parents and students, but they always appreciate it if you make the effort."

In a busy school day, it is very hard to find moments to converse with individuals, and often we only do so to discuss something negative. Use some of the following methods to make communication proactive, rather than reactive.

Some communication tips:

- Keep a list of all of your students' home contact details handy. Be careful not to leave this list in general view.
- Always return phone calls as quickly as you can, as parents might be anxious and they will be grateful for your quick response.
- Keep a communication record. Include notes about any phone calls home and any one-to-one chats with individual students.
- If you have not communicated at all with some students' parents by half-way through the academic year, then make a couple of positive phone calls to 'touch base' with these parents. Parents always love to receive positive phone calls.
- Include a communication box in your classroom. Explain to your students that they can post any concerns, worries or queries into this box, and that when they do so, you will get back to them as quickly as possible. You could provide a pen and slips next to the box with a space for students to write their names, the issue and a place to indicate the urgency level.
- Dedicate two after-school slots a week where you can guarantee that you will be available for students to come and speak to you if they need to.

Teaching tip

Some students struggle to start talking about whatever is troubling them. A good first question is, 'Is it school, home or personal?' It's also always good to ascertain what the student wants. Do they just want to talk the issue through, or do they want your help?

Help!

"When a student needs your help, it is not always immediately obvious what to do."

As a secondary school teacher, you could be approached by individual students and parents/carers to help with a variety of situations. It's tempting to try and provide answers on the spot, but it's better to reflect and consult with colleagues and school procedures before dealing with issues.

There is advice later in this section for dealing with a specific problems students are likely to encounter, but here is some general advice you could follow when dealing with a student or parent who approaches you with a problem.

- At first, listen carefully to the problem (especially in the case of an angry parent – as their anger is likely to subside when they know they are being listened to). Don't interrupt.
- Always take the issue seriously, even if it seems trivial to you.
- Often the person with the problem already holds the solution that is most palatable to them. They have all the details of the situation and are best placed to know if a solution is likely to work or not. If you allow them to talk and listen actively, they will often provide their own solution.
- Note down key details of the problem.
- If you do not have any immediate suggestions, explain that you will talk to your colleagues and seek advice about how best to deal with the situation. Never feel you have to provide an instant solution.
- Many problems disappear when monitored. The attention given to the situation often helps.
- If what is being said is a complaint about you, explain the situation to a senior member of staff.

Safeguarding

"We all receive safeguarding training but it's helpful to be reminded of what to actually do if a young person discloses something to us."

Most teachers will have had some safeguarding training, but it is a good idea to consider and plan appropriate ways of responding, should one of your students make a concerning disclosure.

If a young person discloses information that leads you to believe they might be at risk of harm:

DO

- Where possible and appropriate, use open-ended, rather than closed, questions.
- Listen to the child carefully.
- Provide openings for the young person to talk, and encourage them to speak openly.
- Be extremely sensitive to how the child is feeling.
- Keep the focus on student welfare.
- Explain your concerns using simple language.
- Explain the procedure concerning confidentiality and the need to involve other adults if you suspect the child is at risk of harm.
- Document anything that has been said as fact, opinion, allegation or observation.
- Immediately notify a designated lead for safeguarding.

DON'T

- Interrogate the child with closed or irrelevant questions.
- Expect pupils to share your views.
- Promise to keep secrets.
- Make any judgements about whether the young person is at risk or not. It is always better to just pass the information on.

If a student discloses any information that leads you to believe that they or anyone else is at risk of harm, you must pass on that information to a designated safeguarding lead.

Teaching tip

Research has shown that when a child or young person discloses something, they have usually been building up to it for some time. Because of this, never be scared of frightening the young person off.

Involving parents

It is good practice to tell parents/carers that a disclosure has been made, as long as you judge that it won't put the young person at further risk of harm.

Study difficulties

"Students don't often realise that their "colleagues" are struggling with exactly the same issues."

This activity helps students to share problems and create realistic solutions without exposing any individual's struggles.

Taking it further

Explain that if someone is finding a particular lesson really difficult, they can talk to you about it.

Bonus idea ★

Students could compose a list entitled, 'I study best when...'

Start by asking small groups of students to list difficulties that students might encounter at school. Ask students to consider times when they struggled with learning and why.

You could prompt them with the following list:

- Difficulties with the way a teacher teaches;
- A technique a student struggles with (e.g. note-taking, listening for a long time);
- A subject they find particularly difficult;
- Not knowing what to do when you don't understand something;
- Struggle to read things quickly enough;
- Poor concentration and daydreaming.

Compose a list as a class. Go through the list and ask students to raise their hand when you read out problems they identify with.

In their small groups, ask students to consider advice that might help students with each of the problems listed. The kind of things students might offer include:

- Talking to the teacher about the difficulties;
- Noticing when your concentration fails and trying to address this;
- Doodling to help with listening;
- Clarifying with the teacher what to do when you don't understand something;
- Accepting that everyone finds some subjects more difficult than others;
- Explaining your difficulties to the adults at home and seeing if they can help;
- Asking to sit in a different place in class.

Mediate!

"Occasionally you will need to get involved with conflicts that happen between students because they have not managed to sort out the situation for themselves."

When students are having difficulties with each other, you will sometimes need to step in – even if the conflict is not causing disruption to lessons. When this happens, you need to aim to be restorative and make everyone feel better. The following method for mediating between two parties is effective for de-escalating a conflict.

When two students or groups of students are in conflict or having difficulties, arrange for everyone to meet at a time outside lessons. You might wish for a colleague to join you in the case of more than two students.

Once all the people involved are present, set the ground rules, e.g.:

1) '...one person speaking at a time, and I will indicate when it is time for you to speak.'

2) 'If you get angry, explain you need time to cool down.'

3) 'Everyone needs to listen respectfully.'

Then ask both students the following questions and get them to take turns answering them. Allow students time to respond to what was said, until there is some consensus.

1 What happened?

2 How did what happened make you feel, and how were you affected?

3 What can be done to repair the harm done?

4 What have we all learnt, so as to make different choices next time?

Once students have answered these questions, check both parties feel more positively about the situation and that any bad feeling has gone.

Teaching tip

Be aware that this approach is different from the traditional one that tends to get teachers asking:

- What happened?
- Who is to blame?
- What is the appropriate punishment?

Beat bad behaviour

"There's no magic wand for students who persistently misbehave, but finding the triggers for the behaviour can help."

When a student is in trouble with teachers for disruptive behaviour, you might be called upon to address this behaviour. You cannot accompany the student to every lesson, but you can tackle the behaviour in a generic way in the following ways.

If a child is struggling to behave well in school:

- If possible, organise a meeting with parents/ carers to discuss the issues. Arrange for regular liaison – either by phone call or report card. Encourage parents to offer rewards if the student gets positive reports.
- Be solution focused. Note times when the student does behave and engage with lessons. What is it about those times that help the student to behave?
- Monitor behaviour. Make students aware that you care that they need to learn to manage their behaviour, that it is under scrutiny, and that it disrupts others.
- If the student struggles with their behaviour, help them to recognise when they are becoming angry, and to develop appropriate coping strategies.

Develop a behaviour plan that looks at:

1 What teachers want to see and what helps the student to maintain these behaviours.
2 What happens to first indicate the student is starting to struggle and how to address this.
3 What happens if the student's behaviour escalates? How can staff help de-escalate?
4 What behaviours are you trying to prevent, and what should happen if these behaviours are seen? Share this with all staff who deal with the student.

Anti-bullying

"In an ideal world, every school will have developed an anti-bullying policy involving the whole-school community, so that everyone understands what bullying is and what to do about it."

Your school should have an anti-bullying policy that outlines the necessary procedure. However, below is some general advice about how to best approach incidents of bullying.

When dealing with bullying:

- You need to take any disclosure of bullying seriously and notify your head teacher who will be monitoring all incidents of bullying.
- You need to talk to both the bully and the target of bullying. Sometimes, it can be worthwhile to bring both together and mediate using a restorative approach (see Mediate! page <XREF>) but professional judgement needs to be employed, as this could give the bully more 'ammunition'. However, when successful, the bully can be made to realise the harm s/he has done, and this can prevent further bullying.
- Make it clear to the bully that the bullying needs to stop. If appropriate, you could tell the bully that sanctions (like having to stay in at break times or after school) will be employed if it does not stop.
- You need to involve parents/carers of both the bully and the target starting with a phone call informing them about what has happened. For bullying incidents that have been extremely damaging, meet with parents to discuss what needs to happen.
- You need to support the target of bullying by being available to him or her, should they need to report a further incident.
- After a couple of weeks, talk to the target of bullying and check that the bullying has stopped. Do this again about six weeks later.

Teaching tip

It is important to know what bullying is. Bullying is where one person deliberately sets out to hurt or upset another person, repeatedly and over a period of time. Usually the targets of bullying do not feel like they can stick up for themselves, as there is a power imbalance. One-off incidents of nastiness are unlikely to be bullying.

Homework support

"Homework can cause a lot of anxiety. Few children start secondary school with homework habits that mean homework is never late or parents don't have to nag for the work to be done."

Dedicate some time to supporting good homework habits. Help students to consider how best to approach homework.

Support your tutor group with homework by:

- Discussing how students approach homework and explaining that different people approach it in different ways. Do they do it straight away, or do they leave it until the last minute? Do they need to be reminded by their parents it? Do they have anyone that will help them at home if they get stuck? Do they always get it in on time? Do they really concentrate on it, or are they often distracted by other activities?
- Offering some tutor time to do homework and be available to help.
- Showing a regular interest in how they are getting on with homework. This can be general, such as asking, 'Did anyone do homework last night, and did you find it OK?'
- Discussing good homework habits such as:

  o Make sure you know what homework has been set and when it is due in.
  o When possible, do homework on the day it is set. Alternatively, make plans for when each piece will be completed; write the plan down and stick to it.
  o Allow yourself a short break when you get home, but then get on with your homework.
  o Ask an adult to check over your homework when it is finished.
  o Complete homework in a place where you won't be distracted by anything.

Taking it further

Explore the idea of procrastination with pupils. Give personal stories of procrastination. Ask: What is it? What are the signs that someone is procrastinating? What prevents people from starting and/or finishing work? How can people overcome procrastination? What good does procrastination do in the long run? How can you best overcome procrastination?

o Have a 'Homework station' with pencils, rulers, colour pencil, erasers and sharpeners, etc., so you don't have to waste time looking for these things before you get started.

o Don't keep finding excuses not to do your homework – remember how good you feel when you've done a good piece of work.

o Remember that starting the homework is often the hardest bit. Be determined to get started. The sooner you start, the sooner you will finish.

o Put your homework straight into your school bag when it is finished so you don't forget it.

o If you find a piece of homework really hard, either ask an adult to help or take it into school and ask your teacher to explain what you need to do again.

o If you are struggling to concentrate, allow yourself a ten-minute break and then return to your homework.

o Never start homework close to bedtime. You won't be able to concentrate well, and it might make your brain become over-active so you find it difficult to get to sleep when you go to bed.

Bonus idea ★

Have a homework focus week. In this week students could set targets for developing better homework habits and report back how they are getting on.

Friendship difficulties

"In most cases, it is best to leave students to sort out any friendship difficulties themselves; however, occasionally just a little intervention can help.'

Friendships are important to everyone, and when they go wrong it can cause a lot of stress — especially for secondary school-aged children. When friends fall out, you can occasionally help with some mediation (see Mediate! page 19) or chatting with both parties. Here are some guidelines for such a chat.

Teaching tip

If students are extremely emotional about whatever happened, meet with them separately initially, so you can mediate with all the information before the students talk things through with each other.

When talking to two friends who have fallen out:

- Get both students to take it in turns to state why they have fallen out. Insist that only one person talks at a time and that they listen to each other carefully. Explain that they will both get a turn to speak before they start.
- Focus on helping the students declare how the other's behaviour made them feel. Nobody can argue with how something made you feel.
- Once you have understood what the problem is, encourage empathy by speculating about how the two friends are feeling, e.g. 'I am wondering if X feels let down because...and Y feels sad because...'
- Be solution focused and ask, 'What needs to happen for you to both feel better about each other?'
- Remind the students that they were once friends, and ask them to state something they like about the person. (Unfortunately when some people fall out, they begin to see the person they fell out with as 'all bad' and their good points become insignificant. These people especially need help to see the person is still the same person they used to be good friends with.)

Taking it further

If students manage to forgive each other, ask them to reflect upon what they have learnt from this situation.

Target setting

"As a form tutor, you have responsibility for your students' overall wellbeing and success at school. Setting targets can help students focus upon what they need to get better at."

The most effective target setting is always completed in consultation with the person whose target it is. In a form group, this can be an informal process and focus on non-academic areas, as well as their general approach to school work. Give students a selection of targets from which they are to choose three.

Some example targets that students could choose from include:

- Improve punctuality so I am never late.
- Complete homework on the day it is set.
- Ask for help when I do not understand something.
- Pack my school bag the night before, so I can be more organised.
- Remember my PE kit every time it is needed.
- Write all homework that is set in my home--school book, and make sure I know what I need to do before I leave each class.
- Improve my grades in a subject I struggle with, so I get mostly Bs, instead of Cs.
- Put my hand up and answer teachers' questions.
- Ensure I go to bed at X o'clock and go to sleep to ensure I get enough rest each night.
- Join an after-school club.
- Take care in the presentation of my schoolwork, so that anyone picking up my book would see an improvement.

Teaching tip

Make regular time to review targets. If students think they have achieved a target, encourage them to set another.

Taking it further

Students can also add their own targets, or adapt those that have been given, to make them more suitable if they need to.

E safety

"It's essential to teach young people to navigate technology safely and to develop a discerning eye for what they could be exposed to."

The vast majority of your students will have access to the internet at home. Students use computers for research, interests and for social networking. Visiting (or re-visiting) e-safety guidelines is always time well spent and part of safeguarding your students.

Give your students a copy of the following e-safety advice. Ask them to discuss with a partner the reason why each piece of advice has been given and then feed back.

- Only give your email address and mobile phone number to friends you completely trust.
- Never pass on someone's email address or phone number without their permission.
- Always keep your mobile phone with you or somewhere where nobody else can get it.
- Don't use your real name on social networking sites.
- Never post personal details (such as address, your school name, family details or phone numbers) on a social networking site.
- Never tell anyone your passwords.
- Never reply to nasty messages – save them and show them to an adult.
- Always think twice before you post a photo or video online of yourself.
- Always ask friends' permission before you post a photo or video of them online.
- Never feel pressurised to post a photo or send a message by phone.
- Never arrange to meet someone you do not know through the internet or by mobile phone.
- If you discover a website with information or images that upset you, block it.
- If someone makes you very uncomfortable or upset with what they have written on a social network site, block them.

Community building – activities to help your tutor group bond

Part 3

How well do we know you?

"It's always good to get a group of students to show an interest in each other."

This is an easy-to-use and non-threatening tool that gets your class mingling in a lively way. It does require a little preparation, but once it is set up it can be used again and again. It can even be used with groups of teachers in the staffroom.

Teaching tip

Ideas for other questions include:

- What's your favourite lesson?
- What's your favourite colour to wear?
- What would you most like for tea tonight?
- Which of the following names you'd most like to be called?
- Which museum would you most like to visit?
- Which prize would you most like to receive?

- Before you use this activity, prepare a selection of multiple choice questions and their answers. The questions need to be about a person's preferences and should have multiple answers to choose from, e.g.:

Which of the following would scare you the most?

o A parachute jump
o Holding a tarantula
o Walking in a graveyard at night
o Swimming in shark-infested waters

Or

Which of the following would you rather have as a holiday?

o Lying on a sunny beach
o Walking in the hills
o Skiing
o Visiting a city in another country

- Prepare around eight to ten questions and photocopy them – one for each student.
- Hand out the sheets and ask pupils to select one answer for each question.
- Once everyone has completed their sheets, they must find another person to work with and take it in turns to guess the answers they gave to each question.
- Once they have guessed one person's answers, they can go through the process again with another pair.

Negotiate

"It's fascinating watching a group of students negotiating. A lot of personality exhibits itself!"

This activity starts with individuals, pairs, groups of four, then eight and then should be carried our as a class, in two groups. At each stage, students have to do a simple negotiation and arrive at an agreement. It can teach individuals a lot about how they interact with others.

The activity requires the following steps.

- Ask every student in the class to think what their favourite flavour crisp is.
- Ask students to find a partner and share this information with him or her.
- Next, tell students that they need to decide which flavour they could both eat if they had to agree on just one flavour. For example – if one student chose cheese and onion and the other chose prawn cocktail, they need to agree which one of those flavours would be most palatable to both of them.
- Having agreed the flavour, they need to join another pair of pupils to make a four, share their flavours and again agree on which flavour would be palatable to all of them.
- Continue until the class is split into just two groups and see if the group can agree on one flavour!

Once this activity has been completed. ask pupils to discuss the following:

- Did you find this activity easy? If not, what did you find difficult?
- Did you find giving up your flavour easy?
- What happened when you were faced with a flavour you really did not like?
- How much harder would this activity be if it was about something serious, like a subject you had to have ten lessons of a week?

Teaching tip

You could do this activity with other preferences, or give students a 'menu' of choices from which to choose (e.g. places to go on holiday, pizza toppings). Topics that students might find more difficult to compromise about include: an occupation you have to have for the rest of your life or hobbies you have to do three times a week.

Two truths and a lie

"Voluntary disclosure can always be very entertaining!"

This activity requires minimal preparation and is about helping students get to know each other a little better. This activity can be repeated, either as it is, or by adding a 'theme' to the activity. As the teacher, you can join in too, of course!

Each student needs a piece of scrap paper, about A5 size.

- Ask pupils to write three pieces of information about themselves.
- Explain that two of those pieces of information will be true and one will be false.
- Give students plenty of time to think up information to write. Explain that far-fetched ideas are less likely to be believed – so include unusual things that are true about yourself, if you can. And, with the same reasoning, information that seems very possible is more likely to be believed.
- To help students, you could list the following prompts:

  o pets you have
  o things you got told off for when you were younger;
  o a memory from primary school;
  o an aspiration for the future;
  o a talent you have;
  o a prize or award you have won;
  o a dangerous experience;
  o favourite things – e.g. meals, lessons;
  o things you dislike.

- Once all students have written their truths and lies, they hold them up or stick them to their fronts with sticky tape.
- Ask students to see how many people's lies they can guess. Award a point for each lie guessed.

Bonus idea ★

You could give students a topic that they write their two truths and a lie about, such as family, childhood, opinions about school, hobbies, wishes they would make, etc.

Connect with Venn

"A Venn diagram can be used to help pairs of students get to know each other a little better."

Help students to 'community build' using a Venn diagram. This simple idea gets students asking lots of questions about each other and finding out what they have in common. It can be used repeatedly if you match up different pairs of students.

This activity needs little preparation.

- Put students into pairs and give each pair a large sheet of paper.
- Ask students to draw two overlapping circles on the sheet. Encourage students to have approximately one third of each circle not overlapping and a third of the total area overlapping in the middle.
- Ask students to label one circle with one student's name and the other with the other student's name.
- Next, ask students to complete the Venn diagram. Anything the two people have in common is written in the overlap of the two circles and anything they do not have in common goes on the individual part of their circle.
- If students fail to think of anything, give them some of the following ideas:

  o appearance (e.g. hair colour, eye colour);
  o factual information (e.g. middle name, primary school attended, month/year born in, place of birth);
  o favourites (e.g. colour, animal, band, subject at school);
  o things they hate doing;
  o achievements (e.g. can/can't swim, plays a musical instrument, etc.);
  o cities/towns/countries they have visited;
  o hobbies;

Taking it further

Ask pairs to get into fours and see if they can get any further ideas from students they have not worked with. If both people in the pair do not do something, they could write it outside the circles.

Bonus idea ★

Ask three students to produce a Venn diagram illustrating what they do and don't have in common with each other.

No giggling!

"There's lots of talk about how good laughter is for us!"

Remember how when you were a child in a situation where you really were not meant to laugh, but felt a strong urge to? These activities play on that sensation. Try out some of the following activities with the strict instruction that laughing means you will be disqualified.

Taking it further

Put one student in charge of trying to make as many people smile or laugh in two minutes as they can. A point is awarded for each student who 'cracks'. See who can gains the most points.

Explain to students that you are about to ask everyone to do some slightly odd activities with the aim of making them laugh. Everyone is 'in' at the start of the session, but that laughing or smiling automatically makes you 'out'. The last person to remain 'stony faced' will be the winner. Work through the following activities.

- Say 'ha ha, he he' over and over.
- Tut and roll your eyes over and over.
- Look at everyone in the class sternly and wag your finger at them.
- Say repeatedly, 'My name is... and I like custard more than jelly.'
- Declare: 'This is extremely serious,' constantly.
- Hum a tune you like.
- Fold your arms, look angry and glare at different people around the room.
- Raise your eyebrows while you nod your head a few times and lower them while you shake your head a few times, and then repeat.
- Open your mouth wide and then close it continually.

What's the question?

"Sharing information about yourself can be difficult for some people, but it helps to affiliate groups."

This is an unusual and entertaining way of getting students to share some information about themselves. It involves being given the answer and then working out what the question was.

You need several large sheets of paper. These can be spread around the room. On each sheet there is an answer (see below for suggestions). Explain to students that they are going to write the question that would make the answer true for them personally. So for example, if the answer was 'No, I hate them,' the question could be, 'Do you like Brussels sprouts?' Encourage students not to duplicate questions.

Teaching tip

This activity works better if you also participate.

Allow students several minutes to circulate and write their questions on the pieces of paper. Encourage students to make up a question for all answers, but also explain that it doesn't matter if they miss one or two out.

When students have completed the sheets they want to, you can circulate and read some of the questions and see if you and your class can guess who wrote any particular question.

Answers you might like to use include:

- Every now and then;
- At the weekends;
- Yes, I really like it;
- I'd prefer it, actually;
- I don't have any;
- It always makes me laugh;
- On Tuesdays;
- Yes – it's an ambition;
- I don't think I ever will;
- It's probably my favourite thing to do;
- I find it really difficult.

Secret best friend

"I spent a lot of time trying to work out who it was. I failed completely."

This is a good activity for students who are new to secondary school, and it promotes kindness. It involves allocating an anonymous best friend to each student. They then proceed to do secret acts of kindness for this person.

Taking it further

This activity can be done with staff as well! A good time to do this can be the week leading up to the Christmas break.

Put all the names of your form group's students into a 'hat'. Invite each student to take a name from the hat and check it instantly to ensure they have not picked themselves; make it clear they are to put their own name back and select another if they pick their own name. In the unlikely event of the last person picking him or herself, ask about ten students to return their names to the hat and repeat the process.

Next explain that the person they selected has become their 'secret best friend' and that they need to try and do at least one kind thing for this person this week without him or her knowing who did it. This will probably mean that students will need to elicit the help of others to complete their act of kindness.

Give examples of the kind of things students could do:

- Get another student to deliver a small gift.
- Have someone open the door for the person and see them to their seat.
- Deliver a drink to the person at lunch time.
- Arrange for the person's bag to be carried to a lesson.
- Deliver a written compliment to the person.
- Make something for him or her.
- Leave a pleasant message where they sit.

At the end of the week, ask students to share what happened, and who they suspected was their secret best friend.

Charity work

"Raising money for charities creates a 'real' situation that students can collectively contribute to, and it can create fun opportunities."

Working as a tutor group to raise money for a charity can be a very effective way of getting your students to work together on a meaningful project with a common goal. Creating donations for charity also has a 'feel good' factor.

There are hundreds of charities for which your students could choose to raise money. They could investigate and choose the charities themselves. Then you could ask individuals or groups of students to propose a charity for which they would like to raise money and do a 'pitch'. Alternatively you could raise money for a cause with recent coverage in the media.

There are a number of ways to raise money, and you can ask your students for ideas, e.g.:

- A sponsored activity: silence, skipping, writing, walks, ball bouncing, etc.
- An auction. For things donated by the students and staff, for a teacher to be a lunchtime serving slave or for a homework helper.
- Sales, cup-cakes, biscuits, books.
- No school uniform days, where you pay for the right not to wear uniform.
- Create a humorous school magazine and sell it.
- Create a persuasive leaflet that asks for donations from parents and carers.
- A pamper shop where students can pay small amounts to have their hands massaged, nails painted, hair styled, etc.
- A 'torture a teacher' session, where students can pay to soak, paint, and stick feathers on a teacher.
- Fete-style stalls with small prizes (e.g. treasure hunts, number of sweets in a jar).

Bonus idea

Students could write to large local businesses to ask for prizes, and a raffle could be held for staff and/or parents and carers.

35

Down it goes!

"There is no way this can be achieved unless you work together."

This activity is excellent for illustrating team work. You set your class a simple task and they will struggle to complete it unless they work as a team.

Split your class into groups of about eight people. You will need a reasonably long bamboo cane – one for each group. Alternatively – you could use just one cane and invite each group to complete the task, one group at a time. Set the task:

- Get each group of eight to stand facing you in pairs, side by side, and one pair behind the other (like a queue of pairs).
- Hold the bamboo cane at about shoulder height, so it is between each pair of students. Ask students to hold their index finger up to their side so they are all holding up the cane.
- Before you let go, explain that the students need to lower the cane to the floor but that at all times they must be touching it.
- Watch the students attempt to do this.

Some groups will take longer than others.

Once complete, discuss the following questions.

1 Did you find this activity frustrating in any way? If so, why? How did you deal with your frustration?
2 Did anyone take the lead, and if so, did others let him or her take the lead?
3 Do you think you could have done this without communicating with each other?
4 Were you tempted to cheat, or did you actually cheat at all?
5 What did this teach you about working as a team?

Group gazette

"Sharing information about yourself always helps people to connect."

Create a class book containing a 'fact file' about the students in your tutor group. Students can look at in spare moments during registration time.

Create a simple, two-sided sheet of A4 fact file for students to complete. The kind of things you could include on the sheet are:

- Name
- Birthday
- Primary school
- Best memory from primary school
- Star sign
- Colour of hair
- Colour of eyes
- Names and ages of brothers and sisters
- How long it takes you to walk to school
- An achievement you are proud of
- Pets – with names and animal type
- Birth place
- Hobbies
- A list of favourite and least favourite (e.g. flavour crisps, lesson, meal, drink, TV programme, band, shop, season of the year, holiday, thing to do at home, sport, game, time of day, day of the week, present you ever received, animal, place to eat out)
- Three words that could be used to describe you
- A really early memory from when you were a small child
- What you would like to be when you grow up.

Be careful not to probe students to share anything too personal.

A, B, or C?

"Puzzling preferences can be fun, and children who share the same preferences feel an automatic connection to each other."

This is a simple activity that requires students to share some preferences. It is simple to set up and requires students to move around and learn a little more about their classmates.

Teaching tip

Keep the signs up and possibly add a 'D' so that you can take class votes like this for any class issues you might want to know student preferences for, now or in the future.

Bonus idea ★

After each round, ask students where they think you would stand. Take a vote and see if students get it right.

Print a large, A, B and C onto separate sheets of A4 paper. Position them high up on the wall in three corners of the classroom. Explain to the students that you are going to give them some choices and that they are going to physically demonstrate their preference or answer by positioning themselves near the letter that represented their choice.

Example of things you could ask:

Would you prefer:

- To have a: **a)** banana **b)** chocolate or **c)** strawberry milkshake?
- To play: **a)** cricket **b)** chess or **c)** a computer game?
- To have a holiday in: **a)** a city **b)** a beach resort or **c)** in the countryside?
- Your next lesson to be: **a)** maths **b)** PE or **c)** art?
- To travel to school by: **a)** bike **b)** walking or **c)** bus?
- To travel to school by: **a)** hot air balloon **b)** helicopter or **c)** a white-water raft journey?
- To go on: **a)** a Ferris wheel **b)** bumper cars or **c)** a roller coaster?
- To get directions to somewhere by: **a)** map **b)** someone explaining the route or **c)** someone actually taking you along the route?
- To eat: **a)** pizza **b)** a roast dinner or **c)** chips?
- To be: **a)** an elephant **b)** a lion or **c)** a hippo?

After each round, you could ask students to discuss their preference.

Active learning techniques – tools for exploring different issues

Part 4

Four words

"This is a simple tool that always facilitates involved discussions!"

This technique requires very little preparation and is simple and easy to use. It gets students to discuss issues that you would like them to reflect on. It is effective for making students really consider any topic and the key issues connected with it.

To use the four words technique:

- Get students into groups of four and give each group two pieces of scrap paper.
- Give students the topic or question you wish them to discuss (see examples below) and ask them to write what they consider to be the four most important or significant things about this topic.
- Once the group has agreed upon the four things, ask pupils to duplicate their list.
- Next ask each group of four students to form two pairs and separate from the other pair they have just worked with and go and form a four with another pair. Each group will now have a list of potentially eight things that they believe are important about this issue.
- Ask the newly-formed groups to decide which four of the eight issues are the most important. This creates further discussion – often with new ideas thrown into the pot.
- Ask a spokesperson from each group to feed back their 'answers'.

You could discuss the following topics:

- Happiness;
- Being attractive;
- Friendship;
- Preventing bullying;
- Good parenting;
- What is a good career?
- Preventing prejudice;
- Feeling good about yourself.

Graffiti wall

"The value of a graffiti wall is not just in what is actually produced but in the interactions that happen while it is created."

A graffiti wall can be used to consider any topic. This idea is very simple. You roll a sheet of plain wallpaper across a line of desks or the floor and invite students to add their ideas to it. While students are adding to the 'wall', they should have at least five other people within close proximity who they can interact with.

Plain wallpaper can be picked up very cheaply from DIY stores and can be used in the following way.

- Outline some basic ground rules. People can add anything to the wall, but it must not be offensive to others.
- Roll the paper out so that students can access it from both sides.
- Invite students to come and add words, pictures, labelled illustrations, poems, instructions, reports, cartoons, catchphrases, facts, opinions, lists, quotes, advice, questions, mind maps, flow diagrams, quizzes, headlines. In other words, absolutely anything that relates to the topic.
- Explain that they can interact not only verbally, but also with whatever each person has added to the graffiti wall – as long as the other person is happy for this to happen.
- Once people have added to the wall, ask them to move around it, looking at everyone's contributions. You could suggest students can add things in places they did not originally create, if they wish to, and if they do it respectfully.
- Ask students to find something they did not produce that they agree with and something they disagree with – this will prompt further discussion about the topic.

Teaching tip

Examples of topics that could be discussed using this method include: the ideal relationship, the ideal friendship, arguments, change, prejudice, anger, emotions, what you admire in others, ambitions etc.

41

Quick to draw

"Information goes in pretty well when you're having fun!"

This is a method that can be used to present any type of factual information to your students and you can guarantee, even when the information is not that interesting, your students will still have fun and remember the key points.

It is advisable to do a 'dummy' round of this game as some students may struggle to follow the rules. However, once students have understood how to play, the game can be used again and again for different topics.

You need to provide your students with fact cards — separate cards with different facts on them. Students will need to be in groups of an even number (at least four) and will need scrap paper and pencils.

Explain the following rules:

How to play

1 The aim of the game is to win more fact cards than your opposing team.
2 If there are four of you, you work as two teams of two. If there are six of you, then you work in two teams of three, etc.
3 For each turn, there is one drawer and the rest of the team are guessers. Each member of the team takes it in turns to draw.
4 Spread the fact cards out on the desk, so all the facts can be seen by everyone. The guessers turn away while one of the people drawing chooses one of the cards to draw by pointing at it but not moving it.
5 The people drawing then both proceed to draw the fact that they have chosen. No letters, numbers, gestures or spoken words can be used by the drawers.
6 The first guess is taken by picking up the correct fact card. If the guess is incorrect, then the other team wins that card and the people drawing can continue until the correct card is guessed.

I agree. . . or not

"An agreement spectrum gives you the opportunity to dither while you make up your mind."

An agreement spectrum is just as it sounds — an opportunity to say how much you agree or disagree with something. It can help students to develop their opinions about a variety of issues.

Create and use an agreement spectrum in the following way.

- Make a sign that says 'strongly agree' and another sign that says 'strongly disagree' and put them up on the wall at opposite sides of the classroom with room for students to stand anywhere on the imaginary line that runs between them.
- Make a statement that students will agree or disagree with. This statement can be about anything (e.g. 'Money makes people happy').
- Ask students to stand in the position that indicates how they feel about this statement from strongly agreeing with it to strongly disagreeing with it. They can stand in the middle if they do not have an opinion either way.
- Ask students 'Who would like to say anything about where they are standing?'
- Listen to those who are happy to share a view, and then invite students to change positions if they want to.
- Some examples of statements include:

  o It's hard to stand out from the crowd when you are a teenager.
  o If I saw someone being bullied, I would do something about it.
  o I would keep a ten-pound note if I found it in the corridor.
  o I want to travel a lot when I am older.
  o I am an organised person.

Teaching tip

If someone stands in a position where they are all by themselves, go and stand close to them, as it can be difficult to break from the crowd when you are teenager. You can use this as an example of peer influence and discuss why it feels hard to stand in a place nobody else is in.

Top ten tips

"Creating a top ten tips list for anything requires you to really think about the topic you are creating the tips for."

This method can be used to explore a variety of topics in depth and will result in useful advice to share with your whole class.

Taking it further

For a creative and entertaining exercise, students can make up top ten silly tips for things like:

- Keeping your teacher happy;
- Persuading aliens to come to Earth for a holiday;
- Making a toddler laugh.

Students have to create a top ten tips list for a given topic. It is interesting to give the whole class the same topic and see if they come up with similar advice.

- Give students the topic. Example topics include the top ten tips for:

  o being a good friend;
  o completing homework;
  o getting on with parents in the teenage years;
  o getting the most out of school;
  o for being organised for school
  o for deciding your future career path;
  o for beating stress;
  o for a healthy lifestyle;
  o for making up after falling out;
  o for staying safe when out and about;
  o for getting good at something;
  o for a school to combat bullying.

- Where possible, let students use the internet to research advice that different organisations give on the topic they are researching.
- Don't worry if students don't manage to produce ten tips. They might struggle to do this with some topics.

Whatever issue you are exploring using this method, you will find students simply cannot complete it without really discussing and considering the topic.

Under the hammer

"People can get quite carried away at an auction – even when it's a make-believe one!"

This is an effective exercise in exploring values using an auction. It can be used to explore anything that has a lot of criteria (e.g. qualities of friends). It can take a while to complete, but is very entertaining, and a follow-up discussion is interesting.

Hold an auction in the following way.

- Give all students 100 points each. Explain that these are like currency and can be spent at the auction.
- Have a list of criteria with you (see examples below). It is best if you have the criteria written on cards, so that when a student has a successful bid, they physically receive the card.
- Explain that everyone has 100 points to spend, and that they can bid on anything. If someone bids 20, you can outbid them with 21, and so on. The person who receives the card is the person prepared to bid the most. Acknowledge it is difficult when you don't know what the next thing will be, but state that this exercise works best when people get on and bid.
- Each student needs to keep track of their points. (You can ask their neighbours to check they are subtracting what they spent.)
- Start the auction by taking one criteria at a time, and set the bids rolling.
- Example of criteria include:

  o qualities of a friend (fun, attractive, reliable, honest, stylish, helpful, funny, fit, etc.);
  o things that make us happy (a great hobby, money, good friends, one close friend, a nice bedroom, lots of clothes, etc.);
  o things we would like to rid the world of (anger, war, fast food, global warming, poverty, starvation, pollution, waste, etc.).

Teaching tips

You could ask students to make a list of the things they bid on – whether they were successful or not, as these still give an indication of what values are important to them.

45

World's worst, world's best

"We can learn a lot by exploring the extremes of best and worst!"

This active learning technique gets students to consider the worst possible way of doing something and comparing it with what they believe is the best possible way of doing something. It is an entertaining way of exploring some serious issues.

This activity is very simple. You simply propose the issue you wish to explore and then ask students to either list, perform or makes notes to help them explain what the world's worst and the world's best of this thing would be like.

Examples of issues that can be explored include the world's worst and the world's best:

- Apology;
- Job interview;
- Lesson at school;
- Way of teaching;
- Way of learning;
- Way of comforting someone who is upset;
- Way of giving directions to someone;
- Making a new acquaintance or friend;
- Way of dealing with someone who is trying to persuade you to do something you don't want to do (e.g. smoke a cigarette);
- Way of dealing with someone who has just insulted you;
- Communication with another who has something serious to say;
- Way of disagreeing with someone in a debate;
- Way of completing homework;
- Way of giving advice;
- Teamwork;
- Way of approaching something you find difficult;
- Way of dealing with being angry;
- Way of dealing with worry.

Hot seat

"Being in the hot seat requires students to empathise with a character."

Putting someone in the hot seat gets students to sit on a chair at the front of the classroom and assume a given role. The rule is that while they are in the seat, they must act as that person, and all reactions and responses need to be as if they were coming from that person.

Being in the hot seat requires:

- Empathy;
- Creativity;
- Quick thinking;
- A deepening understanding of the person they are being while in the hot seat.

Examples of roles to explore include:

Light-hearted ideas

- Someone from a nursery rhyme complaining about their lot (e.g. Humpty Dumpty, Little Miss Muffet);
- A well-known fictional character who you can pretend has recently joined the school (e.g. Harry Potter);
- An inanimate object (e.g. plant pot, washing machine etc.);
- An alien who is trying to make sense of Earth.

More serious ideas

- A target of bullying;
- A bully;
- A really wealthy person;
- Someone who is feeling stressed, angry or worried;
- A refugee;
- A homeless person.

When a student leaves the hot seat, give him or her time to come out of role. You can do this by asking an unrelated question, e.g. 'Do you know what you are having for tea tonight?'

Teaching tip

Ideally being in the hot seat should be optional, so to get students started, put yourself in the hot seat first; then ask students to work in small groups with one person in the hot seat; later persuade some of your more confident students to take the seat in front of the whole class.

Bonus idea ★

You could ask students to research a historical character and then ask them to hot seat. This can mean they can answer questions and give factual information.

Recipe writing

"You simply need ingredients and a method, of course!"

Recipe writing can be used either as a creative exercise or as a means of exploring an issue. What is produced is often entertaining to read and can be used to create a recipe book to entertain your tutor group.

Ask your students what is usually included in a recipe (e.g. ingredients and instructions). Explain that you are going to give them a title for which they will write a recipe. You can choose either a serious or entertaining title. Here are some examples to choose from.

Entertaining

- Recipe for a chaotic journey to school (Ingredients might include: a forgotten packed lunch, odd shoes on your feet, heavy rain, etc. Instructions might include: 1) Pick up your sister's bag by mistake before you leave. 2) Call for a friend who is miles out of your way. 3) Discover your watch is 25 minutes out.);
- Recipe for a disastrous lesson;
- Recipe for a terrible sports match.

More serious

- Recipe for a good friendship (Ingredients might include: understanding, the ability to forgive, etc. Instructions might include: 1) Always look happy to see your friend when you meet. 2) Always show concern if your friend is upset;
- Recipe for successfully dealing with uncomfortable emotions;
- Recipe for doing well at school.

Once your students have completed their recipes, you could bind them together to make a recipe book.

Order! Order!

"It's not just the results of an active learning exercise that is important, it's the discussion and consideration that's needed to complete it too."

Putting things in order is a simple way of considering any issue. Whether something is being put in order from most to least significant, or most liked to least liked, students need to engage with the issue. If you ask students to complete the task in pairs, they also need to engage in discussion and negotiation.

Create a list relating to any topic and ask students to simply put the items in order. It always helps if students can cut each thing out, so that they can physically place the items in order. You will, of course, need to give a description of what the criteria for ordering are, e.g. from the most important to the least; from the biggest to the smallest; from the most irritating to the least, etc. You can explore almost any issue with this method, but here are some examples:

Taking it further

When students have become used to this as an activity, you can give them a blank sheet with boxes to fill in, and ask them to create the criteria that someone else is going to use to put the items in order.

- Important to unimportant aspects of school;
- The best things about friendships and the least best;
- Things I find hard to things I find easy;
- Things that annoy me from most to least;
- What I would like other people to think of me – from most important to least;
- Things I worry about – from most to least;
- Ambitions I most want to achieve;
- Things I have to do every school morning – from those I like most to least;
- Things I can do to stay healthy and how easy I find doing them;
- Current news stories I am most to least aware of.

Step forward

"This activity develops more and more empathy as it unfolds."

This activity is simple, yet powerful. It requires students to step into a given role and then consider how the person in that role would answer the question they were asked. If the answer is 'yes', they simply step forward, or if the answer is 'no', they stay still.

Allocate roles to students. Be careful to give students with high self-esteem the less fortunate roles and those with low self-esteem the more fortunate roles.

Here are several roles, but you could make up more. It is interesting to give two different students the same 'character' to see if they respond in the same way!

- You are probably the most popular person in your class. Everyone likes you.
- You are always naughty in class and you never get on with your work. You like to make people laugh, but often people just get annoyed with you.
- You have a best friend who lives in the same street as you, and you have known each other since you were toddlers. You and your best friend are in the same class. You are both quite liked by the rest of the class, but they usually leave you and your best friend alone.
- You are bullied after school by some boys from the year above you.
- You are bullied by some girls in your class.
- You have lots of friends.
- You are teased by almost everyone in the class.
- You and your best friend do everything together, but you are both quiet and do not really mix with the rest of the class.
- You are quiet and try very hard to get things right, but you get upset when you get things wrong, or if your work isn't good enough.

- You are always trying to get people to like you. You care more about what people think about you than what you really want.
- You have a different 'best friend' every week!
- You are always falling out with people and then making up again. You often stir up trouble between other people who are friends by talking about them behind their backs.
- You are more into computer games than having friends.
- You are a very cheerful person and you are always prepared to help people out.

The questions:

1 Do you like school?
2 Do you enjoy other people's company?
3 Does your mum/dad/carer talk to you about any worries you have?
4 Do you rarely get upset?
5 Do you think you are good looking?
6 Do you always have someone to be with during break?
7 Do people listen to what you have to say?
8 Would you feel all right about getting up in assembly and talking to the whole school?
9 Do you work well in a group?
10 Do people want to sit next to you in class?
11 Does your mum/dad/carer and teacher trust you to do things well?
12 Are you good at cheering someone up?
13 Are you enthusiastic?
14 In games, are you chosen quickly to be on a person's team?
15 Do you do well at school in your lessons?
16 Do you rarely get bored?
17 Would it be hard for someone to persuade you to do something that might get you into trouble?
18 Do you like to do nice things for others?
19 Do you rarely lose your temper?

At the end, ask students how they found that exercise. Then ask students to disclose their 'character' to others.

Teen issues
– PSHE-style
activities covering
issues relevant to
teenagers

Part 5

Who am I?

"Understanding who we are, how we differ from others, where we are average and where we are extreme, can be a life-long exploration!"

Most teenagers are very busy trying to fit in, of course, but demonstrating that we are actually all different not only helps us become self-aware, but it also helps us to openly celebrate diversity. This activity encourages students to consider aspects of their personality and how they might differ from others.

Taking it further

There are plenty more ideas of spectra that could be used in this activity that can be found on the internet if you type 'personality spectra' into a search engine. There are also online personality profiling tests that you could encourage students to use to develop greater self-awareness.

This activity explores a variety of spectra along which people can sit at different points of preference. There are many ways to explore each spectrum, such as getting students to stand on an imaginary line to represent where they would put themselves. Alternatively, they could mark this in pencil.

The following are examples of the kind of spectra you could use:

Radar out or radar in people
Are you someone who has a thought and immediately shares it? Are you an expressive person who repeats things for emphasis and talks more than you listen? Do you learn by talking things through?

Or

Are you a person who thinks before sharing your thoughts with other people? Do you listen more than you speak? Do you prefer to learn by quietly thinking about something? Do often think 'you have already said that!' about other people?

Worrier or not?
Are you a person who finds themselves worrying a lot? Do you not like taking risks? Do you often find that what you worried about should not have caused you to worry?

Bonus idea ★

Students could create a personality page with as many answers as they can think of to the question placed in the middle of the page: 'Who am I?'

Or

Are you a person who rarely worries about the possible hazards or difficulties in anything?

Change lover – or not?
Are you someone who gets bored easily and likes changes and novelty and likes to do things differently, if at all possible?

Or

Are you someone who likes things to stay the same and lives by the motto, 'If it ain't broke, don't fix it!'?

Detail or big picture?
Are you someone who likes to think about things in order, tends to think about the present moment, likes things that say exactly what they mean and is good with lots of details?

Or

Are you someone who tends to focus on the future, likes to think abstractly, is quick to see the big picture and gets overloaded with too many details?

Planner or Flexible?
Are you someone who likes to make plans and stick to them? Do you like to be organised? Do you like decisions to be made and kept to?

Or

Are you someone who is flexible or easily distracted? Do you tend to like to keep your options open?

Logical or preference?
Are you someone who makes decisions based simply on 'what makes the most sense' after weighing up pros and cons without feeling too emotional about what was decided?

Or

Are you someone who struggles to make difficult decisions if they have a bad impact on other people? Or do you make decisions based simply on what you prefer?

Advice, please!

"Teenage problems are usually quite niche and often ignored!"

Teenagers have to deal with new bodies, new sexuality, social anxieties, worries about school and conflicts with parents/carers over freedom and responsibilities. This activity airs these problems using a distancing technique, so students can discuss and create advice for their own problems without admitting to any of them.

Teaching tip

After a class discussion, you could put students into groups of four and ask them to create bullet points listing the main pieces of advice they think the person with the problem needs to hear.

Explain to your students that they are going to create a problem page aimed at teenagers over a couple of sessions. Give students some scrap paper and ask them to anonymously write down the kinds of problems they think some teenagers might experience and send to a problem page.

As a prompt, use the following list. Some teenagers have problems to do with:

o friends and friendship groups;
o fitting in;
o worrying about looking good;
o worrying about school;
o arguments with parents and carers;
o growing up;
o girlfriends and boyfriends;
o puberty.

- Ask students to choose one of their ideas and anonymously write a short letter to a problem page.
- Read through the problems and select those which you think would be interesting to discuss in another session.
- Take the problems one at a time, read them out and take suggestions from the students about the advice this person could receive. Discuss the advice and whether or not the group considers it helpful or not.

Taking it further

If problems and advice are collected and typed up, an advice leaflet could be created to be circulated throughout the school. Websites with advice for teenagers could also be added.

Dilemmas

"We all experience dilemmas in our lives, and they often force us to look at our values."

Presenting students with some dilemmas can evoke considerable discussion. A dilemma should have no straightforward or obvious course of action because different choices have different consequences. Looking at different outcomes and why they might be a good idea or not can help students to consider how their values contribute to the decisions they make.

Present students with a selection of dilemmas to consider. These could include:

- You are in the park with a load of mates. One of them offers you a cigarette and teases you for not taking it and smoking. What do you do?
- You borrow your mum/dad/carer's coat without asking them, and when you are out, you rip the coat on a gatepost. The coat cost a lot of money. What do you do?
- You have been invited to a friend's party and have said that you will go. Then, another friend, one you are closer to, invites you to his/her party. You'd rather go to the second party. What do you do?
- You are with a group of friends, walking to school, and they all start saying unkind things about your best mate. What do you do?

Explore these dilemmas by asking:

1 What choices do you have about what you could do as a response to each dilemma?
2 What might happen as a result of making each of the choices available?
3 What reasons are there that would make a person choose the choice they made?
4 What do you think you would do? Why?
5 What values have contributed to the choice you would make?

> **Bonus idea** ★
>
> Students could explore the idea using a spider diagram. They could put the dilemma in the middle of a sheet of paper and draw all the choices available – each on its own 'spider leg', the actions that would be taken as a result of each choice, and the reasons why a person might take each course of action. This information could then be used to consider what might be the best choice.

Peer influence

"There is no doubt that peer influence increases when children arrive at secondary school. Peers step up in status and adults step down in the life of students at secondary school."

Peer influence can be powerful. It can be a positive and a negative influence. Looking at this issue and helping students to recognise and manage it is a really relevant exercise for students at secondary school.

You could explore the issue of peer influence in a number of ways, such as the following:

- Tell students the story of how a teacher in a middle school had asked all the year seven pupils to tuck their trousers inside their socks. These pupils were also instructed to say 'This is the cool way to wear trousers at the moment!' to any younger child from the school who asked about the trousers and socks. Before long, nearly everyone in the whole school was wearing their trousers in this way. Ask your students to discuss this. Why did everyone start wearing their clothes this way? Would it have worked the same way in a primary school? Do they think every child had to actually be told that this was how to wear trousers in school?

- Explain that we often do things because of peer influence. A good example of peer influence is when adults prevent other adults from driving when they have drunk alcohol. Can students think of an example where peer influence might not be so good — especially with teenagers?

- Distinguish between peer influence and peer pressure. Peer pressure would be one person putting direct pressure onto a peer to do something like smoke a cigarette.

Taking it further

If possible, and if you are comfortable to do so, give some appropriate examples of your own teenage years and the things you might have done because everyone else was doing them.

Bonus idea ★

Ask students to consider times when the adults they know are affected by peer influence, and give their opinion about whether they think this had a positive or negative effect.

While peer pressure does happen, peer influence is more responsible for people trying out new things. Peer influence is about doing something because everyone else is doing it, or because you believe everyone else is doing it. (Sometimes teenagers receive an exaggerated view of how many of their peers are actually engaging in risk-taking behaviour. This imagined majority can put pressure on teenagers to feel they should do. For example, teenagers often think more of their peers have tried smoking than surveys reveal actually have.)

- Discuss why peer influence is so powerful. Do we find it difficult to stand out from the crowd? What are we scared of if we do? How does peer influence make marketing fashion extremely easy? Why might teenagers be more susceptible to peer influence than people of other ages?
- Ask your students, 'When is it okay to go along with peer influence, and when is it not?'
- Ask students to produce posters that define peer influence, make people question whether it is a good or bad thing, or promote the idea that sometimes it's a good idea to go against the crowd, especially if the crowd is doing something you don't really want to do.

A culture of compliments

"Teenagers at secondary school are not often known for gushing compliments at each other!"

Compliments are always nice to receive, and when we receive one, we are more likely to give one. Create a culture of compliments in your tutor group by spending time focusing on them.

Ask students to consider compliments they could give to members of their family. Then ask them to go home and give some compliments and report back what happens! For some students (and their families) this will be a strange, unusual and positive occurrence!

You could explore compliments with your tutor group in the following ways:

- Ask students to think about the last compliment they gave someone. Ask them if they feel they often, sometimes, occasionally, or never, give compliments.
- Explore how receiving a compliment feels. Discuss the appropriate response to a compliment. Discuss how you feel towards a person who has given you a compliment.
- Brainstorm nice things you can say to someone (beyond 'You're nice'). Write the compliments on a sheet of paper. Ask students to individually decide which three compliments they would most like to receive. If particular compliments are very popular, discuss why this is.
- Consider which compliments make you feel better, those about appearance, personality, abilities, achievements or comments on friendship/interactions (e.g. you're a great friend; I enjoy spending time with you).
- Role-model giving compliments often.
- Always acknowledge compliments positively when you overhear them.
- Randomly select one student a week and invite other students to anonymously give compliments about this person. Students could write their compliments on slips of paper and give them to you.
- Explore what might stop us from giving compliments.

Whatever!

"It's a difficult, in-between stage of life — neither child nor adult."

The stereotypical teenager is a stereotype for good reason. Each young person's journey is unique but the difficulties many experience in the transition from childhood to adulthood often stem from wanting more freedom from the control of the adults in their lives. Explore these issues with your tutor group and produce material to share with the rest of the school.

Get your tutor group to engage in considering teenage life in the following ways:

- Watch 'Kevin becomes a teenager' on YouTube and discuss how he changes overnight. Although this was created for comic effect, ask students which aspects of this they think ring true.
- Develop and issue an anonymous questionnaire that explores what it's like to be a teenager. Questions to ask could explore: a) how perceptions, wishes, relationships and activities have changed since childhood; b) the struggles and difficulties teenagers have that they did not have as children; c) what they want now that they did not want as a child; d) how the relationship with parents/carers changes when a child hits the teenage years; e) how life will be different when the teenage years are over, etc.
- Explore the transition from child to teenager from parents' and carers' points of view. How is the relationship between a child and his or her parents different from the relationship between a teenager and his or her parents? What adjustments do parents have to make?
- Students could present what they discovered in an interesting way, e.g. poster; leaflet with advice for parents/carers; 'The difficulties of being a teenager,' drama for assembly.

Involving parents

You could send home a questionnaire that prompts discussion about parents'/carers' teenage years between them and their child. Questions could help parents to reflect upon their experiences of the teenage years and what they found difficult and what would have helped and what hindered in those years.

Puberty

"If you are asked to deliver sex and relationships education in PSHE as a form tutor, it can be hard to know what to cover."

Most primary schools cover the physical changes of puberty. However, it is always helpful to revisit the topic with a focus on being sensitive to others during the secondary years.

If you are unsure about what to teach about puberty, the following list will help.

Students should learn or revise:

- The physical changes of puberty;
- How to deal with periods and wet dreams;
- That puberty usually starts between the ages of 8 and 14 – although it can start much later, especially in girls who are athletes or dancers and have a very low percentage of body fat. People can feel awkward about being the first or the last to start puberty.
- That puberty brings a lot of change in a short amount of time, and it is good to talk about any concerns you might feel.
- That puberty can make you feel self-conscious, but you can be reassured that you are the only person that has noticed what is making you feel this way;
- That it is inappropriate to make fun of any changes that happen during puberty;
- That many young people wonder if they are 'normal' during puberty.
- That hormones can make you feel really happy one minute and grumpy or tearful the next. This will settle down.
- That during puberty, young people often start to fancy other people.
- What masturbation is;
- That you need to start to pay more attention to personal hygiene at the onset of puberty.

It's a risk

"Because of a number of factors, the teenage years can be the time when many young people first engage in risk-taking behaviours."

Sex, smoking, alcohol, drugs, poor diet and adrenaline-inducing activities are just some of the things some teenagers take risks with, and some teenagers will take more risks than others. There is a tendency to just tell teenagers not to do something that might put them at risk from harm, but this is not the most effective way of impacting on young people's behaviour.

When considering activities that impact negatively on people's health, it is more effective to use an approach that explores the choices people make, and the reasons why they make them. Consider this approach to health and safety promotion.

For example, when covering a topic such as smoking:

- Do not just tell students not to smoke. This contributes to the idea that choosing to smoke is rebellious.
- Consider all the reasons why a young person might try smoking. (e.g. curiosity; because all their friends are trying it or they think all their friends have tried it; because someone dares them to; because their parents do; because they think it will give them a certain reputation; they want to rebel, etc.).
- Consider the reasons why a person might choose never to smoke and explore the negative impact of smoking. (e.g. cost; health; smell; addiction; speeds up the arrival of wrinkles; just don't like the idea of it, etc.).
- Explore the pros and cons of each decision and, as a teacher, keep judgement out of the discussion. Ask students to consider which reasons they think are good reasons for doing or not doing something, and which are bad.

Teaching tip

Be realistic with risk management. Most young people will eventually have sex and drink alcohol. Teach them how to keep safe, rather than aiming to try and prevent them from taking the risk at all.

Bonus idea ★

You could start a discussion about risk-taking behaviours by asking students, 'Why, when we know that smoking is bad for us, do some people still choose to do it?'

I'm hideous

"Teenagers can be self-conscious and self-critical. Messages from peers and the media suggest appearance is really important."

If the media was our only source of information, there would be a narrow idea of what is considered attractive. Develop an alternative guide to attractiveness to boost students' confidence.

Explain to students that people can make themselves more attractive and that you are not talking about using makeup, styling hair or choosing the 'right' clothes.

Ask students to consider which of the following qualities make a person seem more or less attractive.

- Boasting
- Being apathetic about everything
- Being interested in and supportive of others
- Being rude
- Always talking about yourself
- Giving others compliments
- Always putting yourself down
- Talking enthusiastically about things you like
- Holding yourself up straight when you walk
- Mumbling
- Poor personal hygiene
- A sense of humour
- Scowling
- Being positive and encouraging
- Moaning
- A big smile
- Looking confident
- Being easily persuaded to do things by others
- Slouching
- Being stroppy

Explain to students that, whatever we look like, certain behaviours and expressions will make us more or less attractive.

Hard health choices

"Teenagers often don't consider the damaging effects of poor health choices."

Health education features in a variety of places in the school curriculum. Delivering a generic health promotion session that explores the difficulties some people have when making healthy choices can create interesting discussions.

Give students the following list:

- Smoking
- Drinking alcohol
- Drinking water
- Exercise
- Dental hygiene
- Eating food high in sugar, salt and fat
- Sleep
- Eating fruit and vegetables
- Stress

1 Ask students to write down the choices that relate to each of these health-related issues.
2 Ask students the question: 'If we know what the healthy choices are, why doesn't everyone follow them all the time?'
3 Discuss why some people find it hard to make healthy choices.
4 Ask students which healthy options they personally find the hardest to make.
5 People who do make healthy choices tend to:

- have better concentration;
- sleep well;
- have more energy;
- be much less likely to feel depressed;
- have clearer skin;
- fall ill less often.

6 Ask students to imagine they had a friend who always chooses the least healthy option. How would they persuade this friend to engage in healthier behaviours?

> **Taking it further**
>
> Ask students to set themselves three health challenges to try and keep over the next four weeks. Ask students how they will record how well they will do with these challenges, or you could monitor everyone's progress as a class as this will be more motivational.

Street safety

"The independence that comes with growing up means there is a need to create awareness about how to remain safe when out and about"

With your students, visit (or revisit) some guidance for optimising safety when not at home, or when travelling around.

Involving parents

Students can take these sheets home to share with their parents/carers.

Create an A3 sheet with the following information about staying safe in the middle of it (leaving a large, blank space around the edge). Challenge students to illustrate all of the pieces of advice around the edge of the sheet.

- Always have your mobile phone with you.
- Always let your parents/carers know where you are, and agree a time to get home by.
- Always lock up your bike; never listen to headphones when cycling; wear a helmet.
- If you cycle after dark, wear a high-visibility jacket and remember your bike lights.
- Plan your journeys. Know how you will get to and from somewhere before you leave.
- Whenever possible, always go places with friends, rather than alone.
- Always ring home and ask for a lift if you get stuck. Parents/carers would usually rather come and get you than think you were walking home alone – especially after dark.
- If you travel by bus alone, sit near the driver.
- If someone tries to take something from you, never fight back – just hand the thing over.
- Keep valuables out of site.
- If someone in a vehicle stops and asks you directions, keep your distance from the vehicle.
- If you are out after dark, stick to busy, well-lit streets, where possible.
- If encounter difficulties when you are out, get yourself to a busy place and speak to an adult – preferably someone who is with children, a group of people or in a couple.

Teaching tip

Spend some time helping students to keep risk in perspective. Obviously, some parts of the country have lower crime rates than others, so be sure not to exaggerate the incidents of crime or harm that young people encounter. Most young people remain safe and are never involved in situations where they are affected by crime or harm, but the above measures will help to minimise the risk.

Motiv8

"There are always tasks in life that we struggle to get on with. Staying motivated isn't always easy."

Developing strategies for getting and staying motivated to do a task is a skill for life. Use the following tool to help students consider how to enhance motivation to complete tasks.

Get students to develop an effective motivation strategy in the following way:

- Ask students to write about a time when they were really motivated to get something done. It needs to be something they were successful at achieving, e.g. reading a book; learning something off-by-heart; an achievement in sport; or developing a skill.
- Now ask students to remember the time before they did this thing. What did they tell themselves? What did they say to other people? What did they picture in their head? What did they actually see or look at? What did they feel? What did they actually do?
- Now ask students to think about the time they had achieved what they set out to do and ask themselves these questions again.
- Ask students to note down the answers to these questions. These answers are their effective strategy for being motivated to do anything. If they said to themselves, 'I am going to do this,' if they told someone else what they hoped to achieve, or if they visualised the completed task before they started – then these are the components of their successful strategy, and they can use this to motivate themselves to do anything!

Teaching tip

Demonstrate this method of finding a strategy by talking students through an example of how you get and stay motivated. This will help pupils to understand the process.

Bonus idea ★

Find some quotes about motivation on the internet and display them in class.

Stress and strain

"Learning to switch off and relax helps us to navigate life more easily."

The teenage years can be very stressful on account of hormones, social pressures, increased workload and changing relationships. Learning methods of relaxation can help young people to cope more effectively with the challenges of these years.

Taking it further

Introduce students to some relaxation music. Ask students how it makes them feel. Explain that relaxing music can be found the internet and are another way to become relaxed.

There are a number of ways you can teach students about stress and relaxation.

- Discuss what stress is – the hormonal flight or fight response to perceived dangers. This gears up our bodies for a burst of energy, but this is no good if we don't actually need to fight or run. It can leave us with physical symptoms, like a racing heartbeat, that can cause long-term problems.
- Discuss the feelings and symptoms of stress.
- Ask students to search suggested stress busters online, and create a list.
- Teach students yoga or meditation relaxation techniques such as:

  o Tense muscles on an in breath and relax them on an out breath.
  o Breathing in deeply through the nose and out through the mouth for several minutes. This causes the heart rate to slow down and helps people to feel relaxed.
  o Visualise a circle with a dot on the outside – the dot goes round and up on an in breath and round and down on an out breath.
  o Focus on different parts of the body and, bit by bit, loosen the muscles and relax.

- Ask students to think of activities that help them to relax their mind (e.g. drawing, reading, sport, or playing a musical instrument).

When I grow up...

"Some young people know what they want to do as an adult really early in life. Others need a little more guidance."

Asking students to consider their futures and aspirations and link these to their passions, personalities and capabilities is a great thing to do at any time in a student's school career.

- Brainstorm jobs your students have heard of (including careers of parents/carers). Hopefully there will be careers that students might not have heard of. Add unusual jobs and ask pupils what they think these involve.
- Ask students to explore the government website https://nationalcareersservice.direct.gov.uk and find three jobs they think they would like. Ask students to make notes about how to enter each career – link this to their education and qualifications.
- Ask students to consider how their personalities might impact on their career choices (e.g. are they patient, driven, quick-thinking, sociable, etc.?).
- Ask students which school subjects they like most and how they relate to different careers.
- Ask students to prioritise what they think is important in a career, e.g.:
  - working with people;
  - being your own boss – making decisions;
  - making lots of money;
  - helping people in some way;
  - working alone;
  - being an expert in something;
  - working outside;
  - working in the same place every day;
  - travelling around.

Taking it further

You could create an aspirations board that displays students' hopes and dreams for their futures. This can include more than just their careers. It could also include ambitions, things they hope to achieve and life choices.

Changing for the better

"Changing an entrenched habit is notoriously difficult to do, and the first thing that needs to be in place for it to happen is the motivation to change."

Whether it is to achieve a target, get better at something , or stop an undesirable habit, persistent change for the better can be hard to achieve. Talk students through the following process, which should help them make a change for the better — that is, if they really want to do it.

To maximise the chances of making a positive change:

- Word what you want to achieve in a positive (not a negative) way, e.g.: 'I want to complete my homework on the day it is set', rather than 'I don't want to leave my homework until the last minute'.
- Consider what this change would actually look, sound and feel like. Imagine it.
- Ask yourself: 'Does this change involve others? If so, can they help, or can I do this by myself?'
- Ask yourself: 'What might I lose in making this change? If so, how could I reward myself to replace what I might lose?' (e.g. If you stopped eating chocolate every day, you might feel you really missed the taste.) You could reward yourself by doing something else you really enjoy instead, like playing with a pet.
- Consider how determined you are to make this change, as you need to understand its success depends upon your determination.
- Write down your first step towards making this change and when you will take it.
- Think of the benefits of making this change and visualise how it will make your life better. (e.g. 'My parents won't nag me.')

Assert!

"Some adults struggle with the difference between assertiveness and aggressiveness!"

Teach your students to speak assertively as a good way of communicating, and explain how this can both prevent them from getting into aggressive situations and from carrying out actions that they really don't want to do when being told to do something by another student.

Explain that:

- Being aggressive is when you angrily or forcefully state what you want to happen in a way that upsets the person you are speaking to. When people are aggressive, they think that what they want is more important than what anyone else wants.
- Being passive means you do what someone aggressively asks you to do, even though you do not want to do it.
- Being assertive is about stating what you do or don't want to happen without upsetting the other person.

When you wish to speak assertively, just state what you want to happen. For example:

Person 1 aggressively: Give me one of your crisps!
Person 2 aggressively: No, go away!
Person 2 passively: OK...
Person 2 assertively: No. They are my crisps and I am hungry. I might let you have one if you ask nicely.

Discuss with students why speaking assertively is usually better than speaking aggressively or passively. Ask them to practise speaking assertively in response to an aggressive request like, 'Get off your bike, and let me cycle it down the street!'

Taking it further

Demonstrate passive, aggressive and assertive body language and highlight the differences. Direct some passive, aggressive and assertive body language at one student at the front of the class, and ask how each style makes them feel.

Dealing with insults

"When someone insults another person, they usually want a response."

It would be highly unlikely that anyone could get through life without ever experiencing an insult from someone. Take some time to explore how best to deal with teasing and insults.

Taking it further

Ask students to respond to an insult such as, 'You're rubbish at everything!' in the worst possible way and then the best possible way.

Discuss the following with your students:

- For what reasons do you think someone insults another person? (They are grumpy and they want you to be grumpy too; you did something that upset them; they have learnt that insulting others gets attention.)
- What response is most likely to make them continue insulting someone, and what response is mostly likely to make them give up?

Tell students about fogging.

- Fogging is where you agree with the insult in a calm and humorous way, so that the insult literally loses all its impact. For example, if someone said, 'You can't kick a football!' you would reply, 'No, you're right. I'd better get practising so I can get as good as you!'
- Fogging usually catches the insulter off-guard, because it's rarely the response they expect. It usually makes them give up insulting you.

Tell students the difference between teasing and bullying.

- Teasing is where someone says something unkind, but that you can brush off and forget.
- Bullying is when someone keeps deliberately trying to upset someone else by teasing them over a period of time and makes that person feel like you cannot stand up for yourself.

It's how I feel

"Some people are emotionally literate and others less so. Emotional literacy makes life much easier to manage. The good news is that you can get better at it!"

Emotional literacy is being aware of the emotions you are feeling, understanding what might be causing them, knowing the best way to express your feelings, and knowing a good way to respond to other people's feelings. Some people are far more emotionally literate than others. Spend some time helping students consider how best to deal with a variety of negative emotions.

Start by asking students to consider how they deal with emotions by getting them to think of the last time they experienced a negative emotion (like anger, worry, sadness) and what they did in response to the emotion. Everyone has different ways of dealing with emotions, but some responses are not helpful – like hitting someone when you are angry, or bottling things up when you are worried.

Explain that when you feel a negative emotion, you cannot help the feeling, but you can usually choose what to do in response. For example, when you realise that you are getting angry, you could choose to count from zero to one hundred. Spend some time with students considering what bad and good responses are to feeling:

- Worried
- Angry
- Sad
- Scared
- Bored
- Irritated
- Confused.

Students could make information posters to show their ideas, e.g.: 'If you are feeling worried, you could...'

Teaching tip

Often boys receive the message that showing any emotion other than anger is a sign of weakness. Because of this emotional repression, boys will often suffer negative emotions and never turn to anyone for support – even when they feel dreadful. Make students aware of this, and discuss how boys could be encouraged to share their feelings more.

Loads-a-friends

"Friendships become more and more important as young people move through secondary school."

Spend some time with your students considering how friendships can be different, and that we might turn to different friends for different things. This activity also illustrates what friends can, and often do, do for us!

Taking it further

Ask students to create an advert 'selling' friends.

Explain to your students that you are going to get them to consider friendship by asking them a set of questions that can be answered by the name of a friend. Explain that they might want to use the same friend to answer more than one question, and that is fine, but encourage them to try and think of different people for each question.

Ask students to think of the friend that:

- You would turn to if you were upset;
- You would like to get to know better;
- That you have known since you were little, and with whom you share lots of memories;
- You find interesting to talk to;
- Often makes you laugh;
- Makes you feel good about yourself;
- You would ask to help you if you did not understand some work;
- That you would completely trust with a secret;
- That makes you think about things in an unusual way;
- Is quite different from you;
- You admire;
- Would stick up for you;
- Is reliable;
- That you feel you give a lot of support to;
- You would most like to try out something new with (like a sport, a game, a new skill);
- That you would like to invite to your house.

Discuss why are friends important.

Bonus idea ★

Ask small groups of students to discuss friendships and create three lists: a) What friends should never do; b) what friends should always do and c) what we might expect friends to sometimes do.

I think ... –
exploring and
developing
attitudes, values
and opinions

Part 6

I've changed my mind

"Your opinions can change all the time, depending upon which facts you have received about an issue. Sometimes, when you get more facts, or consider something in more detail, your opinions change."

Sometimes people argue with opinions as if they are facts. It's good to help students understand the difference between facts and opinions, and illustrate that opinions can change, depending on the information we receive. These activities illustrate how this can happen and how it is acceptable for people to hold different opinions about the same issue.

Part A

Read the following 'story' in sections. After each section, ask your students what their opinion of King Kolo is.

Section 1

King Kolo ruled the island of Sava. Most of his subjects thought he was a kind and fair king. He was a cheerful man who liked to laugh and throw big parties for his subjects as he thought it was important that they enjoyed their lives.

Section 2

In the far west of the island, there was a small village called Yarvel. King Kolo treated the people who lived there (the Yarvellians) quite differently from everyone else in his kingdom. He built a huge wall around the village to prevent anyone from trying to leave. The Yarvellians were treated like prisoners.

Section 3

King Kolo kept the Yarvellians separate from the rest of the people in his kingdom simply because they were three times as big as anyone else on the island. He told people that it would be far safer if the two different-sized people were kept apart.

Section 4

The Yarvellians were convinced that King Kolo kept them trapped in their village because he was scared that they would take over the whole island and stop him from being king. The Yarvellians insisted that they had no such plans, and that they just wanted their freedom. Being trapped in their village made them very sad.

Section 5

King Kolo did not want to keep the Yarvellians as prisoners, but when he had first become king, they were allowed to roam all over the island. During this time, many of the smaller inhabitants had been injured or killed. At one point, a Yarvellian woman was arrested for deliberately stamping on sheep. The Yarvellians were adamant that the woman hadn't done anything wrong, and that too much fuss was being made over a few dead sheep. King Kolo was searching for another island where he could build a beautiful village for the Yarvellians to call home.

Discuss how opinions changed during the story, relative to the information that was being received. This can be true of real-life issues, and we should always be prepared to change our opinions if we learn new information.

Part B

Ask your students the following questions, one at a time, and ask for responses verbally.

1 What is the most important thing you learn at school?
2 What is the most important feature about any future career you might have?
3 What is the best age to start a family?
4 What makes a good friend?
5 What is the most difficult thing about being a teenager?

After the question-generated discussions, ask if anyone changed their opinion as they considered the question further and listened to others.

I like that; I don't like that

"It's wonderful how everyone is unique."

Exploring personal preferences illustrates how great it is that we are all different. In fact, it makes the world a richer place.

Taking it further

You could discuss how having different preferences is similar to holding different opinions. Different opinions make life more interesting, and the world might be a bit boring if we all held exactly the same opinions.

Obtain a selection of pictures that show contrasting things within a certain category, e.g.

- Contrasting artwork by different artists;
- The same word written in different fonts;
- Photographs of different animals;
- Photographs of different landscapes;
- Different logos for different companies;
- Different pets;
- Different foods: meals, puddings, fruits, vegetables.

Show each picture, and then place the pictures in different parts of the room; then simply ask students to go and stand by the picture they prefer. Ask students to give a reason for their choice – this can actually be very hard to do as often we do tend to just prefer things.

Ask students if they have given their choice some thought, or just gone with a gut reaction, or gone to the same picture that a friend went to. (If anyone admits to this, explain that we might sometimes do that to stronger affiliate with someone, but that it's better to be true to ourselves!)

Ask students:

Bonus idea ★

Students could write 'I prefer...' statements to make a poem, e.g.: 'I prefer chocolate flavour to banana; I prefer evening to morning; I prefer tigers to lions,' etc.

- If they think there is any problem at all with people preferring different things;
- If they have ever teased anyone for liking something they don't like. Explain that this is not a tolerant way of behaving.
- What the benefits of people liking different things might be;
- How the world might be different if we all liked exactly the same things.

What's important to you?

"There's is no doubt that our priorities change at different stages in our lives."

This activity uses the well-known active learning technique of a 'diamond nine' to explore what is important to your students. It can create discussion in class and at home.

A diamond nine is where you are given nine things to sort in order of importance or significance to create a diamond shape. In other words, the most important thing is placed at the top, the next two most important things are placed underneath, the next three important things on the third row down (this will form the middle of the diamond), under that two things and then the least important at the bottom to create a diamond shape. It is not so much the final diamond that is important but the consideration and discussion that goes into creating it.

Ask students to organise the following into a diamond nine:

- Friends;
- Fitting in and not being laughed at;
- Being healthy;
- Getting good grades;
- Eating well;
- Getting plenty of sleep;
- Looking good;
- Having people to help you when you need it;
- Being kind to others.

Once students have sorted their own diamond nine, discuss any differences and explain why they have placed things where they have with a partner.

Now ask students how they think the diamond nine would be different if their parents had completed it for them.

Involving parents

Students can take this activity home and compare the diamond nine they think their parents will create with the one that they actually do create.

A walk around town

"Of course we all stereotype, however we must make sure we are aware that we are doing it and not allow it to affect how we treat other people.'

This is a simple activity that helps to illustrate that we are nearly all guilty of stereotyping — especially if we encounter few people who belong to particular minorities in our day-to-day life. Simply read the passage below and then discuss the questions that follow.

Taking it further

Consider the following statements with your students.

- We all hold stereotypes in our heads, and they are often based on the majority we know.
- Stereotyping is not a problem unless we consider the stereotype as 'normal', and regard those not conforming to our stereotypes as 'abnormal' and/or treat those who do not conform to stereotype, differently.

Stereotyping can be linked to being prejudiced; If we don't accept or acknowledge difference, we are more likely to have a reaction to it.

You are on your way to town and take the route through the park. Everyone seems to be walking with a spring in their step: a parent with a child having a shoulder ride, a couple hand in hand, dog walkers. For a brief moment, you are a little startled by some youngsters whizzing along on skateboards, skilfully avoiding collision, despite incredibly intricate manoeuvres, but then you find yourself nodding because you are impressed.

Just as you are about to leave the park, you notice a couple sitting on a bench, one quite clearly upset and the other is comforting them. However, you don't want to look like you've noticed, so you stroll on.

The pavement starts to become more crowded as you near the town centre. You have to dodge to avoid a pushchair. The person pushing it smiles at you apologetically. You smile back; you've always thought that it must be hard manoeuvring a pushchair.

You pop into the supermarket. You see a shopper struggling to steer a trolley because it is laden down with children. You take a few moments to grab a packet of crisps and head for the checkout. You notice that the shop assistant looks pretty miserable.

You wander into the newspaper shop next door. You stand in front of the magazine rack. You then realise you're standing next to a friend.

'Oh hello, Sam!' you say, 'Isn't it gorgeous?'

'Yes – couldn't be more lovely!'

'Have you got time for a coffee?' you say.

'No, I must rush home; I'm due to take the kids swimming. Alex'll kill me if I'm late. I forgot to turn up for parents' evening last week, so I'm already in disgrace!'

'Oh well, perhaps another time then,' you say, a little disappointed. You wander home.

Once you have read the above passage, ask the questions below. There is no need for students to give feedback and expose their stereotyping – they can just 'think' their answers.

Bonus idea

Explore stereotypes further by asking students what comes to mind (in terms of gender, looks and behaviour) when they think of:

- A primary school teacher;
- A painter and decorator;
- An old person;
- A couple in love;
- A receptionist;
- A footballer.

A) Details

1 Do you think the narrator of the story is a man or a woman? Why?
2 Was the parent giving a kid a shoulder ride male or female?
3 What did the dog walkers look like?
4 What sex were the skateboarders?
5 Were the couple sitting on the bench a male and a female? Which was crying, and which was comforting?
6 Was a man or woman pushing the pushchair?
7 Was the person pushing the trolley, 'laden down with children' male or female?
8 Was the shop assistant in the supermarket male or female?
10 Was Sam a man or a woman?
11 What stereotyping have you done?

B) General

1 Did you see any disabled people?
2 Did you picture mostly white, black or Asian people?
3 Did you see any gay couples?

Effective discussion and debate

"Often in discussions and debates, people get passionate, then defensive, and then dig their heels in and no learning takes place."

School debates are often about issues that students don't really feel that concerned about. Having a discussion about something that evokes strong emotions is different. Take some time to consider what effective discussion and debate is like.

Taking it further

Ask students to look out for discussions happening on the TV, on social media, or anywhere else, and consider how effective they are.

Ask your students to imagine a discussion between two people who hold strongly opposing views. Students can make up what the debate is about. Now ask students to imagine an effective discussion and an ineffective one. Then ask students to list the attributes of both discussions and their likely outcomes.

Ask to make two lists: 'effective discussion' and 'ineffective discussion'. They might include:

Effective discussion
- Both people take turns to speak and really listen to each other.
- Both remain calm, even when strong views are given.
- Both people develop a better understanding of the reasons for the other's viewpoint.
- Both people agree to disagree, or a shift in one person's viewpoint puts it more in line with the other person's viewpoint.

Ineffective discussion
- Both people are talking over each other.
- Both people become defensive and refuse to receive what the other person is saying.
- Both people become angry or upset.
- Personal insults are given.
- Both views become more entrenched.
- Both people lose respect for the person they were having the discussion with.

Happy, happy?

"Since people have existed, there has been considerable debate about what happiness is and how it is achieved."

People are often asked if they are happy without actually considering what it means. Take time to explore the emotion of happiness with your tutor group in a variety of ways, to develop some interesting and thoughtful discussions.

To consider happiness, you could:

- Ask students to order the following from the most important thing to create happiness to the least important. Students can compare and discuss the order they put things in.

  o Wealth
  o Health
  o Lots of friends
  o Lots of possessions
  o The ability to think positively
  o Pastimes we enjoy
  o Achieving well in lessons
  o A family that loves us
  o Being attractive
  o Being able to deal with worries effectively
  o A nice home.

- Ask students to describe the feeling of happiness.
- Ask students to define long-term and short time happiness.
- Explore quotes and sayings about happiness. Discuss what the quote means and see what wisdom it communicates about happiness.
- Ask students what adverts would lead us to believe we need to be happy.
- Discuss this statement: 'happiness is not just about doing things that give us pleasure; it is also about doing things for a purpose'.
- Ask students if it is realistic to be happy all the time.

> **Bonus idea** ★
>
> You could ask students to devise a questionnaire that aims to investigate how happy people are. They could test their questionnaires out on other students.

We're not equal

"We're not often made to think about how unfairly the world's resources are shared."

This thought-provoking activity helps students to consider how the western world has a standard of living it often takes for granted.

Taking it further

Discuss how this is a metaphor for inequality across the world. Ask students why they think this inequality exists and why it cannot be as easily sorted as the inequality shown above, with all the people in the same room.

Read the passage below and then discuss the questions as a class.

Imagine a room about the size of a classroom with 28 people in it. One quarter of the room is furnished (including a plush sofa, carpet, toys, books, games, a computer and a television). The rest of the room is shabby and draughty and has nothing in it except a few bowls and cups.

In the comfortable corner, there are four people sitting at a table eating a roast dinner. They are drinking water with their meal. They got the water from a tap in the room. They have a pudding too, and all agree it's probably too much to eat. They end up scraping food into the bin. Everyone at the table looks healthy and happy, and they are chatting about television, books and games.

Everyone else is watching them from the shabby part of the room. They have not eaten since yesterday and probably won't eat today. They are drinking water, however, they had to bring their water from a well about half a mile away. The water is cloudy. Everyone looks thin, and ill.

Questions for discussion:

1 In what ways is this room not realistic?
2 How would the people eating feel if they looked at the others in the room?
3 What are the other people in the room thinking and feeling as they watch?
4 If these people were in a room together, how do you think they would behave?

Values or opinions

"We hold certain opinions because of our values, but sometimes we are not overly clear about what these values are."

Interesting discussions can arise out of exploring opinions and values and the difference between them. Our values form the foundations of our opinions and this activity gets students to reflect upon this.

Give students these two lists and ask them if they can work out the difference between values and opinions.

Values people might have:
o Respect for self and others;
o A belief in human rights;
o Tolerance for others;
o The right to hold their own view, as long as it does not impact on others' rights;
o A celebration of the differences between people;
o Adherence to the law;
o The importance of honesty;
o Fulfilling your potential;
o A belief in support and cooperation.

Opinions people might hold:
o Most people get married to have a party.
o All gay people are lovely.
o Drinking alcohol is wrong.
o Eating meat is wrong.
o Using animals to test cosmetics is wrong.
o School uniform is a good thing.
o It's important to always try hard at school.
o War is always wrong.
o People who do not work should volunteer.

Next, students must take one **value** from the list and produce an **opinion** a person with that value might hold. Then ask them to take an **opinion** from the list and discuss what the underlying value might be.

> **Take it further**
>
> You could ask students to write a definition of values and opinions to help highlight the difference between these two things, (e.g: **Values:** Principles or standards of behaviour; one's judgement of what is important in life. **Opinions:** Views or judgements formed about something, not necessarily based on fact or knowledge).

What do we need?

"Often the things that contribute to someone having a successful life are not things that are in the school curriculum."

This 'big picture' discussion activity starts with a simple question, can create interesting discussions, and can help students consider aspects of themselves they might need to develop.

Involving parents

Ask students to go and ask the adults at home the same question: What do they think is needed for a successful life?

Ask students:

If a person were to leave school at eighteen and go on to have a successful life, what knowledge, skills and attitudes would that person need?

You could start the discussion by asking small groups of students to consider what is a 'successful life' and what would and would *not* happen in this life. See if each group can reach some consensus before asking them to make a list of what this person would need in order to achieve it.

Take suggestions from different groups and compose a class list. Ask students to give reasons for the ideas they have put forward. If students struggle, give them a few examples from the lists below.

Knowledge
- Of opportunities;
- Of what keeps us healthy and safe (including mental health);
- Of what healthy relationships look like;
- Knowing rights and responsibilities;
- Literacy and numeracy;
- Knowledge needed to do a job/enjoyable pastime/be engaged in activity;
- To know when conforming is beneficial and when things need to be challenged;
- Self-awareness (knowing your own strengths).

Taking it further

You could ask students to privately reflect upon which of the things on the class list that was created they think they have, and which they might need to develop further. They could also score themselves out of ten for how much of each criteria they believe they have.

Skills

- Good communication skills (e.g. assertiveness, negotiation, compromise, conflict resolution etc.);
- Emotional literacy (e.g. understanding and managing feelings, ability to empathise and the ability to forgive, let go, move on;
- Ability to learn from mistakes, and not be scared to make them;
- Basic life skills (e.g. cooking, budget managing, washing etc.);
- Goal setting for motivation;
- Ability to access help and support;
- Informed decision making;
- Ability to take responsibility for your own actions;
- Minimising risk from harm.

Attitudes and values

- Optimism;
- Aspirations;
- Tolerance and respect for others, including people who are different;
- Self-worth (and confidence);
- A love of and receptiveness to learning;
- Self-forgiveness (we all make mistakes);
- A feeling of social responsibility;
- Discerning eye for the messages we receive from the media;
- An individual moral framework that will guide decisions, judgements and behaviours;
- Respect for the right of others to hold opinions that differ from our own (as long as these views do not impact on the rights of anyone else).

Next, ask your students to try and choose the top three things they think are needed for a successful life and try and create a wise saying from this list, e.g. 'To have a successful life you need...'

Is it wrong?

"We all develop our own individual moral code, but it's good to remain open-minded."

Some people have a very clear idea about what they consider to be right or wrong and are quick to share their opinions. This activity teaches students that issues relating to morality are not always that straightforward.

This activity requires a little preparation.

- Start by giving a few ground rules about respecting other people's views.
- Provide pupils with a set of potential wrongdoings or 'sins'. Make sure you include things that might generate considerable discussion and show differences between students outlooks.
- These 'sins' could be written on separate cards – or students could cut them out.
- Ask students to work in pairs and discuss and sort the 'sins' into three groups: one group for things they consider to be 'always wrong'; another group they consider to be 'never wrong'; and a last group labelled 'depends'.
- Once students have completed their sorting, ask how hard or easy they found this.
- Discuss why some people have put the same thing in different piles. Challenge comments such as 'always wrong' and 'never wrong' with possible exceptions. For example, if a student has put abortion in 'never wrong', ask, 'What if the mother chose to abort because she knew she was having a boy and she wanted a girl?' Discuss how courts and juries are often needed to make these complex judgements. Discuss how one person's beliefs or religion might make them consider something wrong that others do not consider wrong.

Thinking and
creative fun –
activities to
engage students
in creative
thinking and
pondering!

Part 7

IDEA 74

That's unusual!

"Sometimes something is really obvious, but at the same time, really hard to see. And that makes no sense whatsoever!"

This is just a simple, but unusual, not-quite-puzzle that might keep your students guessing for a while.

Taking it further

Ask students to look at a page of text and investigate which letters are likely to be the most and least common. Students could tally letters in different texts and see if they come to some agreement. Students can then look at the 'relative frequency' table of letters on Wikipedia to see if their predictions were close.

Write the following text on the board or hand out photocopies. As it is self-explanatory, leave students to read it and try and work out what is unusual about it.

What is curious about this writing? It has not got anything wrong with it — it is just a bit odd. Most writing is not similar to this. In fact, if you look in many books, you would not find big bits of writing with this unusual factor about it. Is a bit missing, is it looking funny or just unusual? As I said, this writing is not actually faulty at all; it is just atypical. Most adults will work out what is unusual about this in about half an hour, but you might do it in half that. You could work it out in a jiffy if you study this writing and also look and think hard.

As soon as you have found what is unusual about this writing, try writing about 'you' in this unusual way. Hard isn't it?

If students struggle, you could give them the following clues – one at a time:

- Look closely at each word.
- There is something that is not in this text that is in most texts.

and finally:

- Look at the letters.

The answer, of course, is that this text does not include the letter 'E' – which is the most common letter in the English language.

The longest list

"Writing a list stretches my brain!"

Giving students criteria for which they have to compile the longest list can be a challenge. Use the following criteria to see which individual, pair or group of students can create the longest list.

Decide upon one of the following criteria. Set either individuals, pairs or small groups of students the task of trying to think of as many things that fulfil that criteria as they can in a given time limit. Ask groups to swap lists and mark each other's. If there are any queries about whether something is legitimate or not, explain they can ask you.

Suggested lists:

- Sports that use a ball;
- Things that run on electricity;
- Countries in Europe;
- Words that rhyme with...;
- Words that can be made with syllables made from numbers or letters. e.g. B4, NRG, 2;
- Animals that are herbivores;
- Nursery rhymes;
- Shop names;
- Famous people who are dead;
- Names beginning with S;
- Capital cities;
- Mini-beasts;
- Things that could fit in a match box;
- Names of flowers;
- Mammals found in Britain;
- Words beginning with K;
- Occupations;
- Things we mix together;
- Things that come in pairs;
- Things that come in lots of different colours.

Bonus idea ★

Ask students to think of some criteria for which lists could be written, and set these as a task on another day.

Memorise it!

"I didn't think it would work, but it does!"

This is a tool that uses visualization to help people remember lists of things. It is extremely effective and has uses in day-to-day life, as well as for revising school work.

Ask students to memorise a list of twenty objects, e.g.:

o mirror
o cow
o ladder
o moon
o teapot
o grass
o table
o gorilla
o elbow
o bicycle
o key
o hippopotamus
o ruler
o candle
o envelope
o lipstick
o T shirt
o rabbit
o box
o flower.

- Ask students to list the objects in order. Most students will only be able to list fewer than ten or so of the objects.
- Suggest the following memory method. Ask students to visualise each object interacting in some way with the next object on the list, e.g. there is a mirror and a cow walks up to it to look at its udders. The cow then climbs a ladder to the moon etc. More unusual images are more effective. Give students time to visually connect all twenty objects, and then see if they can list them in order.

Proverbs

"There's a lot of fun you can have with proverbs."

There are a variety of activities you can do with proverbs. You could use the well-known proverbs below, or use the internet.

Explain that a proverb is a small, well-known saying that gives a wise piece of advice. Give your students two or three proverbs each, and ask them to put the advice into their own words.

Some well-known proverbs:

- People who live in glass houses should not throw stones.
- A bird in the hand is worth two in the bush.
- Too many cooks spoil the broth.
- The early bird gets the worm.
- Beggars can't be choosers.
- Beauty is in the eye of the beholder.
- Many hands make light work.
- Don't count your chickens before they hatch.
- Birds of a feather flock together.
- You can lead a horse to water, but you can't make him drink.
- You can't judge a book by its cover.
- The grass is always greener on the other side of the fence.
- Don't put all your eggs in one basket.
- A watched pot never boils.

You could also ask students to:

- Create a short story ending with the proverb.
- Illustrate the proverb.
- Look for proverbs from different countries and see if their meaning matches or is similar to any English proverbs.
- Draw a humorous 'spot-the-difference' cartoon of someone following the advice next to someone not following the advice.

> **Bonus idea** ★
>
> Ask students to look for more proverbs and see if they can find any that appear to be giving conflicting advice (e.g. many hands make light work; too many cook spoil the broth).

Pass it on!

"This activity can really get students thinking!"

This activity is a puzzle where students need to devise a way of 'transmitting' information to other students, so that only the students they worked with can receive the information (and appear to be able to read minds). This requires a lot of teamwork.

Explain the task to your students in the following way.

- You are going to work in fours.
- One of you is going to pass on to the other three the name of an animal.
- You are going to eventually do this in front of everyone in the class, and only the people in your team should be able to work out which animal it was you 'transmitted'.
- You will agree as a team how to do this using codes, speech, sounds, actions, etc.
- As an example, you might transmit letters, one at a time, and you might choose to transmit vowels in a different way to consonants.
- You might include 'red herrings': things that you do that are nothing to do with the letters you are transmitting, but that might confuse someone who is not in your team (e.g. touching your nose or blinking obviously).
- Work out how you will transmit and practise it several times, so that you are sure it works.

Once everyone has worked out their method of transmission, get groups to demonstrate communicating the name of an animal. Get them to demonstrate several times (different animals) and see if anyone else in the class can work out the method.

Observation

"You can shock yourself with how you don't notice some things that you see every day!

Test the observation skills of your tutor group by using everyday objects to get them thinking about how much we do and don't notice. Some students will be surprised by how little they notice about common everyday things.

Hand out a piece of scrap paper to each student and then give your tutor group the following observation test. Students are to write their answers individually.

1. How many sides does a 20p piece have?
2. What colour is the classroom door and room number (anything on the door they cannot see from inside the room)?
3. Do you notice anything odd about this?

> I love to
> go to the city in the
> the springtime.

4. Starting with a red signal, what are the four further changes a traffic light makes – in order?
5. Which road sign has a triangle with two corners at the top and one at the bottom?
6. What colour are the eyes/shoes/trousers of a teacher known to all students?
7. On its logo, is BBC written in capital letters?
8. Where is the zero on a mobile phone keypad?
9. Apple logo – is there a bite taken out of the apple on the left or the right?
10. What colours is the Google logo?

Mark the answers as a group and compare scores.

Students could then make up three of their own observation questions and hand them in so you can make another test.

Taking it further

There are clips on the internet that can be used to test students' observation skills. Use one of these with your form group.

Bonus idea ★

Give students copies of different pictures, and ask them to write down ten questions that can be answered by simply looking at the picture. (e.g. What colour was the man's coat?) Ask students to work together to show their picture for a set amount of time to someone who has been working with a different picture, and then see how many questions the tested observer can answer.

I have control

"Imagine being able to control things that are usually uncontrollable."

This activity mixes creative and logical thinking, and the result can be used to create a humorous display. It requires students to consider what they would like to control with their own 'magic' remote control.

Taking it further

The ideas your students develop could be used to create a display of 'the ultimate remote control' for the group.

Explain to your students that they are going to be given an imaginary remote control. On this control there are three types of 'control'.

- On/off buttons (like a light switch);
- Buttons that increase or decrease something (like volume buttons);
- Dials that tell you the magnitude of something (like a thermometer or a dial to display altitude).

Give students small pieces of paper with a picture of each type of control on it for them to write their ideas on. Once students have understood the nature of the different 'controls', ask them to decide what they would like each button to control, or dial to display. Give the following examples:

- An on/off button could make it day or night; make you invisible or not; make a friend appear.
- A button that increases and decreases something could control: temperature, the difficulty of schoolwork, the intensity of your emotions, speed time up or slow it down, change the speed with which you are travelling,
- A dial could indicate: how near a parent was to your bedroom; the likelihood of you getting told off; how correctly your work is.

Ask students to try and think of one of each type of control and write their ideas down. Sharing these ideas can be very entertaining!

Ordinary, extraordinary and extra-extraordinary

"This was a very funny activity!"

This is a creative and entertaining activity with a simple method for evoking creative thinking and will give some students the opportunity to demonstrate their creativity.

At the start of the session, define:

- Ordinary – as something that is not in any way remarkable;
- Extraordinary – as something unusual or unlikely, but possible, and;
- Extra-extraordinary – as something that is impossible.

Start by giving students an example sentence:

- Ordinary – I walked down the stairs.
- Extraordinary – I leapt down the stairs, four at a time, and finished with a somersault.
- Extra-extraordinary – I took 0.3 seconds to get down the stairs on my hover-skateboard.

Next, ask them to create their own three sentences, starting with a very ordinary sentence. If students are struggling you could give them the following sentences, or pair them up in mixed abilities.

Ordinary sentences:

- I ate my dinner with a knife and fork.
- I took my dog for a walk round the park.
- I put my coat on because it was cold.
- I combed my hair because it was knotty.
- I played a game of catch with my friend.
- I rode my bike really fast.
- I stayed in a nice hotel.
- I trained my dog to sit and lie down.

> **Bonus idea** ★
>
> Ask students to produce three pictures illustrating their favourite ordinary, extraordinary and extra-extraordinary sentence.

97

Excuses, excuses!

"Exaggerated excuses can be both creative and hilarious!"

This is a simple format for encouraging creative thinking. Students can have a lot of fun with this because there are few rules in the creation process. It involves making up ridiculous excuses and then trying to outdo them with even more ridiculous excuses.

Taking it further

Students could illustrate their favourite excuse.

In this activity, students have to lie and exaggerate their excuses to the point of being absurd!

- Start with the common excuse of why homework was not handed in. Give the example that the dog ate it (which is ridiculous in itself). Then give a further example that shows how the excuse can get even more ridiculous: 'I did it last night, but a pack of wolves turned up and ripped it to shreds because I had drawn a picture of a rabbit on the front of my book'. Give a further example: 'My dog found it interesting, and he was reading it this morning. It would have been mean to have grabbed it off him, just so I could hand it in on time'.
- Let pairs of students create excuses of their own. Encourage them to be as creative and ridiculous as they like, as long as it explains why the homework has not been handed in.
- Decide as a class which three excuses are the most creative and ridiculous.
- In other sessions give students the following scenarios to work out excuses for. Start with a realistic excuse and get more bizarre.

    o I am sorry I was late for school but...
    o I could not wear my school uniform today because...
    o I will not be in school tomorrow because...
    o My hair looks like this because...
    o I have to wear this hat because...

Hands

"Some of the best ideas start with a simple question!"

If an alien landed on earth and wanted proof that most people have a dominant hand, how would you prove it? Pose this question to your tutor group and then leave them to solve the problem.

For this activity you can provide your students with just paper and pencil, but the activity can become more involved if you also provide scissors, offer to photocopy anything they produce, bean bags and buckets, needles and threads, paints and paint brushes, timers and anything else that requires dexterity to operate.

If students are short of ideas, you could draw from these ideas to help them.

- Colouring or painting in the same shape with different hands;
- Writing with left then right hands;
- Cutting a shape out with both hands;
- Carrying out an aiming task (e.g. how many bean bags you can get in the bucket);
- A difficult catching task with both hands – which hand caught something the most times?
- A timed dot-to-dot activity (with the stipulation that the pencil must hit each dot);
- Timing how long it takes to thread a needle with both hands;
- Testing and typing with different hands;
- The time you can balance a stick upright in each of your hands;
- A Jack straws type game – picking up a stick without moving another;
- Using a toothpick to move peas – time one hand and then the other;
- The electric 'hoop along the wire' buzzer game!

Ask students to collect all the evidence they have gathered that proves that one hand works better than the other for most people.

> **Bonus idea**
>
> Get students to present their evidence as if they were demonstrating to the aliens (the class become the aliens)!

Anagram hunt

"Students can become quite involved in making up hunts for other people."

This activity involves students making up a set of clues – each of which leads to a letter. These letters can then be un-jumbled to make up a word or phrase. It can be carried out over a couple of sessions.

Teaching tip

Make a couple of example clues for a couple of letters in your room before you set students off to make their own to make the process extremely clear.

Explain to students that they are going to make up a 'hunt' for other students. Give the following instructions.

- You need to start with an eight- or nine-letter word. Some students might need to use the internet or a dictionary to help them find one they like. Explain that this activity will be easier if they choose words without really unusual letters in them like Q, X or Z

- Next explain that students will use 'letters' around the classroom and create clues that lead to them. For example, 'Look for a sign telling you what to do in case of fire; you need the third letter on this sign'. Or 'Look at the only poster in this room with blue on it; you need to collect the only green letter on that poster', etc.

- Set students off looking to create their clues. They can write these in note form. Once they have written eight or nine clues, ask them to type or write them up neatly, so that other students can follow them.

- These clue sheets can then be swapped, so that students go in search of anagram letters. Once they have all the letters, they need to work out their anagrams. If students have given clues for a nine-letter phrase, rather than a word, they need to put the letter spacings on their clue sheet. For example:
  __ __/ __ __ __ / __ __ __ __

Wordplay

"This game can be played again and again, and you can see your students getting better at it as their methods of deception improve."

This simple game is fun and vaguely educational! You will need a large dictionary – the larger the better! It can be played by putting the whole class into groups of three. It does require some setting up, but once students have understood how to play it, it is easily set up to play another time.

How to play:

- Before the session in which you will play this game, choose about ten unusual verbs, adjectives and nouns from the large dictionary that students are unlikely to have heard of. Give one word with its real definition to each group of three. Explain that they need to keep this real definition secret.
- Explain to the groups that once they have organised themselves, each person in the group will read out the word and give a definition for it. One of these definitions will be the correct one and two will be made up. Explain that the class will vote upon which definition they believe to be true. If most votes go to an incorrect answer, the team beats the class, but if most votes go to the real answer, the class beats the team.
- Give the groups time to work out their false answers. They will need to make sure nobody overhears that their fabrications are untrue, or an indication of which definition is the true one.
- Once the groups are ready, call them up to the front of the class, one by one, to play their round.

Teaching tip

Before you ask the class to make up definitions, demonstrate some made-up definitions of your own for a given word. Ask students what makes a definition believable (usually not too unusual or weird) and what makes it unbelievable.

Media –
developing a
discerning eye
for the media

Part 8

What messages!

"Young people can receive a constant stream of unhealthy and messages from the media."

This activity aims to challenge some of the unhelpful messages students are drip-fed from magazines and adverts. It involves making posters that explore and challenge these impressions.

Taking it further

Take the discussions this activity promotes further by asking the following questions.

- How can the media leave people with a poor self-image?
- How does the 'average' person compare with the media images?
- How might the media leave people feeling terrible about their lives? Etc.

You will need a selection of glossy magazines for this activity, and each pair of students will need a sheet of A3 paper, scissors, glue and felt-tipped pens. Explain that students can choose any of the listed ideas to explore (see below). Students can use images and words from magazines to create a poster that shows their discoveries in response to the question they chose.

- **What would these magazines lead us to believe is 'normal'?** Consider each of the following: attractiveness, ability/disability, weight, age, hair, skin, financial success, possessions, clothes, ethnicity, stress, lifestyle, happiness, ambitions, house, family, friends, leisure interests, emotional state.
- **What is the stereotypical advert person?** Create such a person in the middle of a large sheet of paper and add a few labels that point out a few details about him or her.
- **What is 'attractive?'** Create an illustrated list of rules that the adverts would lead us to believe make a person attractive. Use details about face, makeup, clothes, hair, weight, shoes, jewellery. Don't forget to mention the use of computer enhancement.
- **How do the media make people behave?** What does it pressurise us to do? What does it make us think we need? How could it make us feel dissatisfied or want to be different? What can it make us feel guilty about? How does it encourage people to get into debt? How might it affect eating habits?

Newsworthy?

"It is good to remember that the media only report stories that will grab people's attention and sell newspapers. Sadly, this often means that we get an exaggerated view of negative things happening in the world."

Unfortunately, the media often report stories that are quite extreme, shocking and therefore sometimes overlook all the positive things going on in the world. This creates a very biased view of the world. Explore stories in the newspaper and discuss why they have been reported.

Explore what a newspaper considers newsworthy by:

Taking it further

Discuss with students the reason why they think there are more negative stories in a newspaper than positive ones.

- Selecting a few news stories from a newspaper for your students to look at;
- Giving students the following list and asking them to decide why these stories are deemed newsworthy by the media.

Stories in the newspapers tend to be:

- o Shocking;
- o Have an interesting twist or angle;
- o Make you feel sorry for someone;
- o Be about a celebrity;
- o Be about unusual people;
- o Really tragic;
- o Scare us (this is called 'scaremongering');
- o Evoke a strong emotional response;
- o Involve a large number of people that can be interviewed;
- o Be 'exclusive' to that newspaper;
- o Be about a crime has been committed – especially violent crime;
- o Can last several days or weeks.

Bonus idea ★

Ask students to write an incredibly un-newsworthy story from their daily life to illustrate the contrast of what appears in the news to what happens in most people's lives.

- Discuss the idea that the media can give us a distorted view of the world we live in. Ask students to list some adjectives that describe the impression these stories give us. How different is this world from our day-to-day life?

Headlines

"You can have a lot of creative fun looking at newspaper headlines."

Newspaper headlines are designed to grab the readers' interest. They are a unique 'genre'. By looking at headlines, students will get an understanding of how the media's main aim is to sell newspapers by hooking potential buyers in with snappy, attention-seeking headlines. You will also give them a sense of how different types of newspapers report the same story.

Collect and give students a selection of headlines from a variety of newspapers. Choose from the activities below:

- Get your students to guess what the story is about from its headline only.
- Look at the style of headlines. Ask why the following headline is unlikely to be found in a newspaper: *An old lady was walking her dog in the park when she noticed that a lamppost had fallen across some electrical wires and a nasty accident could have happened.*
- Ask students to look at headlines and notice the key features about them (e.g. short and snappy; use wordplay or rhyme; use a 'hook'; are witty, etc.) Ask students to try and make up some headlines for the following stories:

  o A child of ten manages to do a maths calculation in two minutes that a university professor struggled to do in half an hour.
  o A supermarket accidentally sold thousands of cans marked as baked beans that actually just contained water.
  o A woman broke the world record for the number of flies swatted in five minutes.

- Consider the difference between tabloid and broadsheet headlines. Compare the different headlines for the same story, and use these comparisons to make generalisations about the newspaper the headline came from.

Bonus idea ★

Ask students to turn headlines into long and detailed sentences about what happened. Encourage students to be creative and include as many details as they can.

Different points of view

"Journalists don't hang around to get the full story. They write their reports quickly and often don't have all the facts and might be acting on only one person's version of what happened."

Stories in the media can be very biased, and it is a good idea for students to develop a questioning attitude to what they read. Help your students to develop a discerning eye for what is written in newspapers with the following activities.

Explore how newspapers stories are reported and look for bias by:

- Looking at a tabloid newspaper. Look for reports that seem to be blaming someone for something bad happening, criticisms or implied criticisms of groups of people. Ask students to consider the other side of the story, or how the paper could make some people feel prejudiced towards a group of people.

- Giving your students a copy of the same story reported by a broadsheet paper like the *Guardian* and a tabloid paper like the *Sun*. Look for differences in the way the story has been reported. Aside from the style of writing, how have the people in the story been portrayed? What do the reports want us to think about the people, or the event that has been reported?

- Developing details about a conflict between two neighbours (e.g. a conflict about noise pollution). Make up the details about the neighbours — what they are angry about and what has happened. Ask one set of students to write the report a reporter would write if they had only spoken to one of the neighbours and the other half of the class to write the report that was written if the reporter had only spoken to the other neighbour. Read the reports to illustrate bias.

> **Taking it further**
>
> Discuss how bias has occurred in the writing of history, depending upon who wrote it. Use examples to illustrate bias, e.g. How would Native Americans and White European settlers have reported the colonisation of the Americas?

Fame and fortune

"Lots of young people dream of becoming famous. There is an assumption that it will create a wonderful life."

Spend some time exploring the aspiration and reality of being famous to help students really consider whether it would be a realistic and worthwhile dream to have.

Taking it further

There are some quotes about *being famous* that can be found on the internet. Discuss the messages these quotes give us about being famous, and whether they are positive or negative.

Consider fame by asking students the following.

Part A – fame
1) List some famous people and write what they are famous for next to them.
2) Is there a stereotypical famous person? If so, what are they like? What do they spend their time doing? How do they treat other people? What are their personalities like? What are they famous for? Where do we get this stereotypical idea from?
3) Do you think it is easy to become famous?

Part B – the media and famous people
1) What kind of things have you heard the media write about famous people?
2) The paparazzi can get a lot of money for a single photograph of a famous person doing something silly or outrageous. How does this impact on the lives of famous people?
3) If you were really famous, what kind of things would you no longer be able to do easily?

Part C - Fame and happiness
1) Do you think lots of adoring fans would make a person happy forever?
2) Do you really think fame and fortune is guaranteed to make a person happy? Explain your answer.
3) Why do you think many young people aspire to become rich and famous, even though for the vast majority it is an unrealistic aspiration?

Adverts

"Adverts are persuasively powerful. They obviously work, or companies would not spend the fortunes they do on making them and paying TV companies to air them."

It is an interesting exercise to explore how adverts work and the variety of ways they get us to buy something — even things we don't really want sometimes. You will need a selection of adverts from magazines and newspaper to complete this activity.

Start by asking students what the purpose of adverts is. Hand out the selection of adverts and ask students to consider the method each advert is using to try and persuade us to buy whatever it is they are selling. For example adverts might:

Taking it further

Ask students to create an advert that uses as many of these methods as they can fit into it to sell a made-up product (e.g. a toothpaste called 'Bright').

- Suggest that everyone else is using the product so that we want to join the crowd;
- Make us feel guilty (e.g. imply that we are a hopeless parent or that our home will be full of germs) if we don't use their product;
- Highlight what is great or unique about the product;
- Claim that the product is better than competitors' products;
- Repeat the name of the product several times to put it into our heads;
- Use facts and statistics to persuade us that we need the product;
- Use an eye-catching picture to hook us into the advert.

Discuss adverts further by asking students:

1 Have you ever bought something because you saw an advert for it?
2 Which of these methods works best to persuade *you,* personally, to buy something?

Topical

"Young people don't always understand what is involved in some of the major stories that hit the news, even though they have seen and heard a lot of information from a variety of places."

Even though many news stories cover controversial and sensitive issues, discussing them in a tutor group session will mean your students will develop a better-considered view of current affairs than if they are not discussed at all. Take time to talk about some of the 'bigger' stories and issues that are currently in the media using the following guidelines and points for consideration.

Teaching tip

When exploring any news story, you can start by asking, 'Why is this news?' This question will extract the main issues relating to the story (see also **Newsworthy**, page 105). Another good question is: 'What impression is the reporter creating about this story with the way they have reported it?'

Some general guidance for discussion of current affairs:

When the media covers a sensitive issue extensively

Shocking stories about different crimes or tragedies have regular coverage in both news programmes and newspapers, and this can give people a distorted view about the prevalence of these crimes and/or tragedies. Young people need help to put such stories into perspective: To do this they need to understand that:

- The number of communication links available mean news reporters can tap into a wealth of newsworthy material from around the world with incredible speed, and therefore the viewer receives a highly-distilled version of worldwide violence. The images we receive bear little resemblance to the average walk around our local community! You can discuss this contrast with pupils.
- The media frenzy surrounding a particularly horrible story can give us an exaggerated view about the likelihood of being the victim of crime.

Taking it further

With major world conflicts, students could be asked to investigate what originally caused the conflict.

Explore all viewpoints/choices

When discussing any story in the news, it would be wrong, as an educator, to ever say or imply there is consensus around certain issues, when in fact there is not. As a teacher, giving 'one side of any story' is professionally negligent. Many individuals and organisations hold differing values and opinions, including the media. The teacher's duty is to facilitate discussions about the stories, exploring all points of view.

Facilitating discussions

The fundamental educational task when discussing current affairs is to help students think for themselves and to clarify their emotions and values about any story or issue.

They therefore need skills in:

1 Choosing between alternatives;

2 Listening and reflecting before coming to a conclusion;

3 Abiding by rules and conventions of mutual respect and civil argument.

It is therefore appropriate to use the following questions when exploring a controversial issue:

- Have you always thought that?
- What would count as evidence for or against your point of view?
- What are the actual facts that we know, and what are opinions?

Bonus idea ★

Ask students to see if they can find a news story that is reporting something positive that has happened.

General
knowledge
– activities
with factual
information to
improve general
knowledge

Part 9

Which language?

"How many languages can you greet a person in?"

This straightforward activity that gives students an introduction to a variety of languages and how different they can sound.

Teaching tip

There are many aids to pronunciation on the internet.

Taking it further

Discuss with students what Esperanto was and what it aimed to do. Discuss why students think it did not really become a common language.

First of all, ask students if they know how to greet someone in any language other than English. List their responses. If you have any bilingual or multilingual students, ask them how to greet people in the language/s other than English that they know.

Give students the following greetings. Explain what transliteration is (to represent a word using our native letters to replicate the sounds made when the letters of another alphabet have been put together to make a word). Explain that some of the following greetings are transliterations. (Can they guess which ones?)

You could also give students the list of languages separately, and ask them if they can guess which greeting comes from which language. Check that students know which language comes from which country. When most people have matched each greeting to a language, go through the answers.

Bonus idea ★

Ask students to investigate the letters of different languages and what writing in different languages looks like. They could have a go at replicating a few.

Guten Tag – Good Day - German
Hei – Finnish
Aloha – Hawaiian
Dobry Den – Czech
Shalom – Hebrew
Konichiwa – Japanese
Ciao (chow) – Italian
Dzień dobry (Jen Dobri) –Polish

Zdravstvuyte (-zd-RA-st-vu-y-te) Russian
Sawubona – Zulu
Hola – Spanish
Bonjour – French
Hallo – Norwegian
Gia'sou – Greek
Merhaba – Turkey
Sah wahd – dee – Thai

When was that invented?

"I don't really know the difference between one hundred years ago and five hundred years ago."

Get your students thinking about how technology has changed over time by asking them to put a list of objects in the order in which they believe them to have been invented. Extend the activity by asking them to estimate the year in which they think each thing was invented.

Give pairs or groups of three or four students the following jumbled-up list of inventions or pictures of the inventions and ask them to order them from the thing they think was invented first to the thing they think was invented most recently. You could provide students with a time line (from 1500 BC to the present day) on which to place each item.

Taking it further

Students could use the internet to investigate how early models differ from more recent ones.

Bonus idea ★

You could give your students examples of fashion from different periods in history (e.g. medieval, Tudor, Stuart, Georgian, Victorian, Edwardian, twenties, forties, sixties, seventies, eighties, current) and ask them to sort them into chronological order.

Inventions

- Telephone
- Glass
- CD
- Telescope
- Aeroplane
- Spectacles
- Paper
- Printing press
- Mobile phone
- Steam train
- Bicycle
- Windmill
- Camera
- Car
- Television

Answers

- Glass 1500BC
- Paper 105
- Windmill 600
- Spectacles 1289
- Printing press 1455
- Telescope 1608
- Steam train 1804
- Camera 1816
- Bicycle 1817
- Telephone 1876
- Car 1886
- Aeroplane 1903
- Television 1926
- Mobile phone 1973
- CD 1982

When students have put everything in order, talk them through the correct order. Explain that the first model of anything that was invented would look quite different to the modern equivalent – if it still has one.

Left or right?

"It is surprising how many young people do not understand the basics about left- and right-wing politics."

Students' knowledge of politics varies, usually depending upon how much they have learnt from their parents and carers.

- Ask students what their understanding of taxes is. Explain who pays tax and what this money is used for in this country (e.g. education, the NHS, etc.).
- Next describe two the fictional countries below.

In Beeland, people pay taxes to the government once they earn over a certain amount of money. The government decides how this is spent – paying benefits to low-income families and funding for hospitals and schools, so that medical care and education are free for everyone.

In Ayland people pay very little of the money they earn in taxes. They have to pay private companies for their health care and education. This is fine for the rich people, but hard for the poorer people.

- Ask students the following questions.

1 Which country would a person who did not earn much money rather live in?
2 Which would a big earner rather live in?
3 Which country do you think is fairer?
4 Which would you prefer to live in? Why?
5 Which of these countries is has a left-wing government and which has a right-wing one?

- Explain that people pay more tax in some countries. High tax-paying countries are described as being 'welfare states'. The welfare state tries to ensure that everyone can get health care and education, and poverty is reduced. Other countries have low tax rates and the state provides a lot less.

When was that then?

"It's quite good to have a basic knowledge of the timing of different periods in British history. It helps the details of history make sense."

This activity is about periods of British history. It can be linked to the activity, 'When was that invented?' (page 119) so students understand what the different periods of history were like.

Give students the following list of the periods of British history and ask them to attempt to put them in order. They could do this by placing cards on a timeline.

- The Dark Ages
- The Victorians
- Medieval times
- The Stone Age
- The Tudors
- The Edwardians
- The Iron Age
- Roman Britain
- The Stuarts

Answers

- The Stone Age (before 2000 BC)
- The Iron Age – (c. 650 BC – 43 AD)
- Roman Britain (43 AD – c. 410 AD)
- The Dark Ages (c. 410 AD – 1066)
- Medieval times (1066–1485)
- The Tudors (1485–1603)
- The Stuarts (1603–1714)
- The Georgians (1714–1830)
- The Victorians (1830–1901)
- The Edwardians (1901–1910)

Next, ask and discuss the following questions:

1 Why do you think the Dark Ages were called the Dark Ages?
2 Why do you think the earlier periods of history were not named after the monarchy?
3 What do you think the c. might mean?

Taking it further

Students can add major events to the timeline such as: the Battle of Hastings (1066); the Magna Carta (1215); the Hundred Years' War begins (1337) and ends (1453); the Black Death strikes (1348); Henry VIII becomes king (1509); Elizabeth 1 becomes queen (1558); the gunpowder plot (1605); the Civil War (1642–1651); the Great Fire of London (1666); the first Prime Minister (1721); the Battle of Trafalgar (1805); the Battle of Waterloo (1815); Victoria becomes queen (1837); The First World War (1914–1918).

Bonus idea ★

Students can look on the internet for pictures of houses, clothing and artefacts from each period of history.

Animal trivia

"You can have a good guess at the answer to most animal trivia questions!"

Give students some animal facts and trivia. Ask them to try and remember them. See how much they remember by having an animal general knowledge quiz!

Give students the following pieces of trivia.

- The animal known as the King of the Jungle is the lion.
- The bird with the largest wing span is the albatross (up to 3m).
- The heaviest snake is the anaconda.
- African elephants have larger ears than Indian elephants.
- The world's largest mammal is the blue whale.
- A horse produces about 10 gallons of saliva a day.
- A cat sees about six times better than a human at night.
- A mongoose can kill snakes.
- The fastest land animal is the cheetah (it can run up to 65 mph).
- The largest land animal is the elephant.
- Flora and fauna are names given to plants and animals.
- A cow's stomach is split into four sections, so some people say a cow has four stomachs.
- The tallest dog is the Great Dane.
- The name given to creatures like rats and fleas that can harm people's health is vermin.
- The smallest bird is the hummingbird.
- The fastest sea animal is the killer whale.
- The longest poisonous snake is the King Cobra
- A horse's size is measured in 'hands'. A hand is about 4 inches in length.
- The largest carnivore on land is the Polar Bear.
- The fastest flying bird is the peregrine falcon.
- The longest snake is a type of python.

It's legal

"It's interesting to see when the law thinks you are old enough to do different things."

This activity can start as a general knowledge quiz and move on to a discussion about responsibilities and growing up.

Give students the list of activities and ask them to guess at what age the law says they are legal.

Answers

• Become a blood donor	17
• Choose your own doctor	16
• Go into a bar and order soft drinks	14
• Buy a pet	16
• Have a part-time Saturday job	15
• Apply for a private pilot's licence	17
• Get married without your parents' or carers' permission	18
• Have sex with consent	16
• Be charged with a crime	10
• Buy fireworks	18
• Buy alcohol	18
• Serve on a jury	18
• Move out of your family home with your parents' permission	16
• Vote in a general election	18
• Play the national lottery	16
• Adopt a child	21
• Get a tattoo	18
• Start learning to drive a car.	17

Taking it further

Discuss how having a legal age for being allowed to do something might make it more attractive to some young people to try it.

To take discussions further, you could ask:

1 Did any of these legal ages surprise you?
2 Why do you think these laws are made?
3 Do you think any of these laws should be changed?
4 As you get older, what changes would mean you might be in a better position to be trusted to make more life choices?

Place name detective

"There are lots of clues to be found in the place names of villages, towns and cities in Britain."

This activity requires students to look at a map and place names to answer questions.

Taking it further

Ask students to investigate the origins of the names of further well-known British cities.

Give students the following information and questions about place names in Britain:

aber – means the mouth of a river
pool – Viking for harbour
cwm – Welsh for valley
glen – Scottish for narrow valley
wick – Viking for bay
kirk – Viking for church
thorpe or **thorp** – Viking for secondary settlement
ton – old English for a settlement
cester and **chester** – Roman fort
bury, borough, and **burgh** – old English for a fortified enclosure (like a fort or a castle)
field – old English for open land and a forest clearing
ford and **forth** – old English for a river crossing

1 List some places with the name *aber* in them. Are they at the mouth of a river?
2 Do places with the name *pool* in them have a harbour?
3 Are places named *ford* located at a river crossing?
4 List places with the name wick, *kirk, thorpe* and *thorp*. What do these suggest about where the Vikings settled in Britain?
5 Names with *field* and *ton* in them come from Old English. This implies these places existed when the Doomsday book was written.
6 Find proof that some towns with *cester* or chester were Roman settlements.
7 List some towns and cities with *borough, burgh* or *bury* that still have a castle in them.

Historical fame

"Misunderstandings and confusion about historical figures can be surprisingly prevalent in young people!"

This exercise considers what people were famous for before the entertainment industry went global and viral!

Give students the names of historical figures and ask them what they think each person is famous for, or give the names and the list of reasons for fame and ask them to pair them.

William Shakespeare   Famous English writer who wrote plays (born 1564)

Mahatma Gandhi   Leader of Indian independence (born 1869)

Charles Darwin   British scientist who proposed the theory of evolution (born 1809)

Winston Churchill   British Prime Minister during the Second World War (born 1874)

Charles Dickens   English writer of novels like *Oliver Twist* (born 1812)

Christopher Columbus   Italian explorer who travelled to the Americas (born 1451)

Ludwig van Beethoven   German composer (born 1770)

Florence Nightingale   British nurse who reformed nursing during the Crimean War (born 1820)

Pablo Picasso   Spanish painter (born 1881)

Martin Luther King   American civil rights campaigner (born 1929)

Cleopatra   Queen of Egypt (born c. 69 BC)

Taking it further

Ask students to list as many people as they can who they know are famous for something that is not to do with entertainment, e.g. The Prime Minister.

Bonus idea ★

Ask students to choose a person on this list to find five interesting facts about.